Aviation Tales & Tails

by

Joey Uliana

Printed and published by Hibernation Publishing

Text & cover copyrights © 2021 by Joey Uliana.

The Library of Congress has cataloged the paperback edition as follows:

Uliana, Joey.

Aviation Tales & Tails / by Joey Uliana - 1st U.S. ed.

p.   cm.

Summary: Stories that have happened during the author's aviation career

ISBN 979-8-9850569-0-7

[1. airplanes   2. countries   3 anecdotes]

For more information contact hibernationpublishing@gmail.com

Printed in the United States of America

10 9 8 7 6 5 4 3 2 1

ACKNOWLEDGEMENTS

Thanks to all my friends, who created paths, and even to the antagonists, who created obstacles throughout this journey. Life is a big classroom filled with lessons. You either learn and graduate to higher levels, or you don't learn and are fated to repeat the lessons.

Special thanks to Rick Werner, Marcio Froelich and Connie Martinez, friends who offered me their broad-minded analysis and editorial skills. My gratitude for the existence of Lisa Tarko, my lovely partner in life, who shares her views and intensifies our ideas and ideals.

What's written in this book happened nearly the way it's turned out in print. I needed to change some names to preserve people's privacy, as well as convert some of the locations. I couldn't have made-up the stories, and couldn't have depended on my memory to remember every detail either. On that note, thanks to my primary teach (Mrs. Teresa), who instructed me to keep a journal to write the wonders life has to offer.

This book is dedicated to you, who think you can't accomplish your dreams, that for some reason (financial, physical, or family related) you don't stand a chance against the world.

Believe me, **you can**.

All you need is someone to tell you, "**You can**."

Contents

CHAPTER ONE

The First Wall

You will hit a wall. As a matter of fact, you'll hit many walls, some walls harder than others. Everybody does. There's no way around it. If you envision yourself not having any problems in life, let me save you a lot of frustrations by letting you know that the only time your life will be trouble-free, is when you no longer have a life. No walls, no learning.

My parents say that one of the first words I learned to speak, as a newborn, was not the traditional "mamma" or "dada." It was "paaaane," (translated from the Complete Vocabulary of Baby Words as "airplane" or simply "plane"). The word was usually followed by my tiny right index finger pointing to the rare airplanes that crossed the skies of our small suburban town in southern Brazil.

How early can you recollect events from your childhood? How far back can you remember? Scientists believe that our first clear memories stick permanently in our minds when we are 3 ½ years old. That's when the hippocampus, the segment of the brain used to store memories (not the grounds of a university for hippopotamuses), reaches enough development to do its job.

My memories seem to be even more premature. I can recall the figure of a small airplane that would come to our town once a year, fly circles over a cemetery that was located downtown, and drop something in it.

Later I learned that the airplane was piloted by a local lad that had moved 500 miles from his single mother's comfort and care, solely to fulfill his dream of becoming a military pilot. During his training, in the Air Force Academy, his mom suffered heart complications and died, leaving him with no other close family member. Thus, every "Finados" (the day the locals pay respect to those who have gone ahead of them) no matter where he was, the pilot would make the trip back to his hometown to honor his mom and shower her tomb with petals of white roses.

That image is as clear to me as if it were yesterday.

There are people who spend their entire lives trying to realize what they want to do with it. I, on the other hand, knew right from the start what I was going to be. The only problem was that between me and my dream, there were many cemented brick walls with the word "IMPOSSIBLE" carved across them.

I pushed against that wall as hard as I could; it did not yield a millimeter. I punched it until my knuckles bled; I yelled at it, karate kicked it, thrust my face against it and let a river of tears make it even more real.

It seemed that every brick had been personalized against my goals. One had "no money for lessons" engraved on it, another had "no acquaintances with an airplane," another one in the corner read, "no history of anyone in the family having such aspirations." But the one in the center was the hardest one, three deeply carved letters that hurt the most: Dad.

I remember my mother highlighting how I was attracted to airplanes, only to be followed by my dad's disdain. He hated the flying machines more than anything. I thought that his contempt resulted from his aspirations for me. He had made it clear to everyone that I was going to either become a professional soccer player or inherit his profession as a beverage distributor, just as he had inherited it from his father.

When I turned six, we had a representative from one of the big alcoholic beverage companies come to our house and announce that my dad had won the "Distributor of the year" award.

I was impressed by the man's shiny spanking new car, his mellow manners and his impeccable light beige businessman suit.

An ant would have a lot of fun sliding down the silky fabric.

Like she did to everyone that showed up in our house, my mother graciously invited him to stay for dinner. I felt that he was about to kindly refuse the invitation, when the aroma of her food quickly changed his mind, "It's very kind of you, madam. I'd be honored."

They were having an animated chat over dinner when Mr. Corporation turned his attention to me and asked, "And you, Junior? What are you going to be when you grow up? Are you going to follow your dad's footsteps?"

Back then, many kids would recoil in shyness by adults' questions. Not me, and definitely not to that question. I had the answer on the tip of my tongue, "No, Mister. I am going to be an airplane pilot."

"An airplane pilot?" Repeated the man, surprised by my determination.

My swift confident smile was shattered by my dad's retort, "Oh, stop with this stupid idea, Junior. The sooner you realize it is not going to happen, the better for you."

The gruffness in his voice surprised Mr. Corporation more than my answer.

He looked at my dad and asked without losing his composure, "Why? I mean, an airplane pilot is unquestionably a noble occupation."

3

"It's just not going to happen." The look on dad's face meant that the case was closed and nobody, not even the CEO of the company that employed him, would convince him otherwise.

It's not fair. I thought, trying my hardest not to succumb to the tears that were welling up in my eyes. My dad would clip my ear if he saw me crying, especially in front of a guest. He was a firm believer in the principle of "real men don't cry."

I was eight years old when I heard on the radio that the local airport would be hosting an Air Show. The perspective of witnessing a show in the sky topped anything I had ever wanted. Knowing what my dad's reaction would be, I went straight to my mom and asked her to talk to him.

By his body language, when they were talking, I knew the outcome. When he left for work in the morning, mom delivered the big "NO!" And since he was not around, I sat on the floor, bent my skinny legs together, covered my face with both hands and started crying quietly.

"Juuunior... you know your dad." Mom reached to comfort me. It was hard for her to see me so miserable.

"Why does he have to be so mean?" I said between sobs.

That was not true. My dad was not a despicable person at all; if anything, it was the other way around, he worked hard to provide everything he could to his family. The fact is... children will never know what prompts parents to behave the way they do, until they become parents themselves.

"It's not as if he doesn't love you." Mom said. "He does. He just wants to... protect you."

"Protect me?" I unburied my head and looked her in the eyes, "From what? From being happy?" At that time, I didn't even know what sarcasm was, or that I was using it.

That's when mom decided to tell me the long-kept secret behind his actions. Dad was a young adult when Jordan, his best friend, dragged him to the local airport for one of those sightseeing flights. He had never been in an airplane and feared heights, but Jordan was persuasive enough to convince him; it also had something to do with a "C'mon! Don't be a chicken," comment. Dad had never been an adventurous type, but his macho Italian blood got him in more mischiefs than he likes to admit.

When they got to the airport, the pilot of the tiny sightseeing airplane told them that the weather was not cooperating much, and besides, in order to keep it affordable, he had to fill all three seats. In other words, he needed one more paying passenger to fill the last seat.

They hung around the airport for half an hour and when dad suggested that it was time to go home, a couple pulled in, anxious to go on an airplane ride. The pilot said that the weather was not very good for flying, but maybe it would get better over the town. Now, the problem was that he had only one seat left because Jordan and dad were already waiting. The couple didn't want to fly separately, so dad wasted no time in offering to give up his seat in the airplane. Jordan didn't like the idea at all and proposed a coin toss.

"I have a coin," the pilot said, getting out of his pocket a one-dollar coin.

"But I don't really want to go. You do." Dad protested.

"If I lose, I can go another time." Jordan said, "Besides, you're the one who hasn't flown yet."

Dad finally agreed with the coin toss and called it, "Tails."

The pilot flipped the coin, which seemed to float for a full second, before giving in to gravity.

The coin landed on the pilot's left hand and he covered it with his right hand before dad and Jordan could see which side was up. He, then, made a tiny gap with his hands so that he could see inside. He looked up, gave my dad a weird smile and said, "It's Heads!"

5

Before they had a chance to confirm, the pilot slid the coin into his pocket.

In a matter of minutes, the pilot, Jordan and the couple were strapped inside the little Piper. Dad saw how excited his best friend was at the copilot's seat. As the airplane started taxiing to the runway, Jordan was holding the control steering wheel with his left hand and had his right-hand thumb sticking up, beside an ear-to-ear smile.

Dad saw the aircraft take off and make a left turn toward the city. It looked like a scene in a movie.

He was taken aback when the airplane was suddenly swallowed by the clouds.

Did the pilot intend to do that? How can one see anything inside a cloud? The flight will not be as scenic as advertised. As all these thoughts were rushing through his mind, he heard the engine noise getting louder, as if the airplane was coming back.

Nothing could have prepared him for the next scene, when the little airplane came out the clouds almost in an upside-down position, its nose pointed down and spinning. People say that dramatic events seem to happen in slow motion. Well, this one didn't. In a split second, the ground seemed to elevate to meet with the upturned aircraft, which exploded on impact, less than two miles from where dad was standing, killing everyone instantly.

Things normally don't make much sense to an 8-year-old, but when my mom finished the story, my heart filled with compassion for my father.

"You see... it's not cruelty, Junior. The feeling is actually fear." My mom continued. "He has already lost his best friend to the skies... and now, he's afraid of losing his best son."

6

CHAPTER TWO

Wings to Imagination

Being sympathetic to my dad's loss, I set my dreams aside, and instead of focusing on things related to flying, I put all my energy into sports. I was going to be a football player (football, as in soccer).

Dad was still an avid football fan at heart, reminiscences of a time he was considered the best full back of the local team. Alas, a common knee injury crushed his own aspirations permanently (something that would be an easy fix nowadays, but in yesteryears orthopedic medicine, was a solid reason for someone to 'hang up his cleats').

Countless hours during four straight years were spent either in a football pitch or a futsal court. And since practice makes perfect, I developed all the best qualities of a right-wing player: speed, skills, vision of the game, precise crosses and perfect bending shots. My team won all local and state tournaments and suddenly, we found ourselves getting ready to play the National Junior Championships.

There was a great deal of excitement among us because we knew that there would be a dozen scouts in the bleachers, ready to pave our way up to a professional club.

The team played well in the first three matches and next we

were going to face the favorites, the squad that had won the contest in the previous two years.

Proving that their rank didn't daunt us, we scored a goal early in the first half and the adverse scoreboard disconcerted them so much that they looked more like a rookie team than the defending champions. We were dominating all corners of the field and a few minutes before halftime I almost scored the second goal with a bending shot that hit the right goalpost, traveled over the entire length of the goal line, bouncing off of the left post to the keeper's hands. During half-time, my teammates commented that although it was not a goal, my shot would likely make "the play of the week" list.

We returned to the field for the second half filled with confidence.

Then, it happened.

Fifteen minutes before the end, our midfielder sent a long ball to the right flank of the pitch. I left the first defender eating dust and as the second one started to slide tackle me, I chipped the ball over him, making him miss his target altogether. During the wild sprint I could see, with the corner of my left eye, our striker running far, almost parallel to me, lifting his left hand, as he rushed toward the goal. It would be business as usual for me, a simple crossing for his easy header and the victory would be guaranteed.

That is, if it was not for the sudden emergence of a Piper Cherokee Six flying over the stadium. Typically, one would hear the sound of the engine before one could catch a sight of the airplane. Not this time; the airplane overflew the stadium like a stealthy falcon surveilling an unsuspecting desert rat. My concentration abandoned the ball and followed the airplane from one side of the stadium to the other, its windshield sparkling in the sun, until it was gone. Needless to say, that was enough time for the entire defense of the opposite team to catch up, push me aside and steal the ball.

I can't explain how, but the uproar of the whole stadium was gone, as if it had been stolen by the fading roar of the plane's engine. It was one of those moments like in movies when life seems to move in a blur. My peripheral vision revealed two things. To my left, our striker with both arms in the air, like a castaway on island who failed to get the attention of a passing by ship, and to my right, our coach leaping like an irate maniac on the sidelines.

I simply stood there, feeling like an impostor. Yes, I was betraying something, but it was not my team... it was my dream.

I don't know who was more shocked with my next move, my teammates, my coach, or myself. I lifted both hands high in the air and rotated them, a sign asking to be substituted.

The coach wag on me right away, "Did you pull a muscle? Are you hurt?" He asked as I walked off the field.

"Nope. I just want to be subbed."

"Are you out of your mind, KID?!" Mr. Coach was not happy, "Are you going to give up because of one lapse?"

"It's not that."

"There are at least a dozen scouts here! Do you know what this will do to your young career?" His voice was threatening.

"Which career?" I didn't wait for him to answer it; I just walked the stairs toward the locker-room.

And that's how my short football journey ended, with the coach dropping me at the local bus station, "Why are you doing this, kid? You got talent; you know that."

"I agree sir... and I am going to put it to good use."

My teammates won that game but lost the championship game (without me). Years later, I found out that two of them were invited to join the academy of a professional football club and eventually made to the big leagues. I was proud of them.

I got off the bus, collected my bags and saw my dad far away, leaning against his car. Since I had not called him to pick me up, I assumed that the coach did. His face had "disappointment" written all over it. His eyes followed me to back to the car. It became pretty clear why people call it 'eye contact,' I could feel them poking a hole in me. He finally moved and opened the trunk so that I could throw my stuff inside. He slammed the trunk in a way that tested the car's shock absorbers, his eyes still locked on me, his lips pressed against each other, making it look as if he was holding his breath.

Thirty seconds into the drive and he finally grumbled, "Why?"

"I don't know, dad. All I know is that I want to fly."

"What?!" He slammed on the brakes at once. Good thing no one was tailgating us. "Is that what this is all about? This ludicrous 'flying' talk, again?" One could feel the exasperation in his voice. I didn't feel like having an argument because I knew I'd lose. I only had one thing to say.

"It's my dream."

Instead of yelling at me, he fixed his attention back on the road, cleared his throat a couple of times in a way that resembles a volcano on the brink of an eruption. "Forget about it!" He cleared his throat once again, put the car in gear and we started moving again, "Starting tomorrow, when you're not at school, you'll be at the company."

I opted to nod instead of rebelling. There's a place and time for everything, and besides, I had a plan that I knew he would not dispute.

Instead of working at the company, I found a couple of little jobs here and there: delivery boy, tutoring, and aviation lineman; anything that could help me save money to achieve my goal.

Three months after I started juggling school with three other jobs, we were all sitting at the dinner table and I caught my dad staring at me. I was worried about what he was going to say, and I prepared for the worst.

"Turns out that one of my clients is a private pilot."

I lifted my eyes by reflex, without lifting my head. *Did he just said the word 'pilot' or am I imagining things?*

"Who?!"

"Cosmos. He flies gliders and airplanes."

"Wow!" I lowered my tone. I didn't want to come across as being too anxious. I knew he would change the subject quickly if I did so.

"He is also crazy, I suspect. Can you believe he breeds flies?"

"He breeds flies?"

"Yep... he has a frog farm," dad continued.

"Wait a minute. He is a pilot that owns a bar and a frog farm?"

"Yep, sounds crazy, right?" He said while wildly moving his arms about in typical Italian style.

"What does he fly?" I decided to see how far this could go.

Dad let a gasp of air escape on impulse, "How would I know?"

For a second, I thought I had "crossed the line" when I asked him about the type of airplane, then abruptly he said, "Why don't you ask him?"

"What?"

"He is low on inventory and made a big order. I must deliver it tomorrow. Do you want to come along and meet him?"

Was my dad offering me a chance to meet a real pilot?

I couldn't believe my ears. Or maybe this was a trap, a way to make me start working in the company with him.

"Yes!" I didn't want to sound too excited, but failed miserably, "Of course I do."

He nodded, "Okay...you come to work early in the morning with me, and we'll meet him, after a couple of deliveries."

Despite being utterly mystified, I strived to keep my composure and managed to say, "Thanks dad." Maybe this was his way to lure me to his business, but it was well worth the risk.

He nodded and concentrated on his plate, while mom, also

failing to disguise her contentment, gave me a discreet wink.

Cosmos was not your average Joe. He was tall and thin as a palm tree. He had a complexion that had seen its share of hours in the sun, hair parted in the middle creating two big waves, and he wore those mirrored aviator sunglasses, even when indoors. Before dad was able to introduce me, he stepped forward, flashed his million-dollar smile and extended his hand, giving me a handshake that I felt for days.

"So, you're going to be a pilot?"

There was no hovering around with Cosmos, he was direct and to the point, and I was completely caught by surprise. I didn't know if I should shush the guy, answer him with the same candor or look for the blood that had drained from my dad's face.

Time was up and after detecting my timid nod, he pressed on, as if he had been hired to write down my life's plots for the next couple of years.

"Have you been studying aerodynamics?"

"No, sir... not yet, I don't have the books and..."

He interrupted my formality without formality, "Drop the 'Sir.' First, I'll give you some aviation literature to get you up to speed, and then we can plan an introductory lesson where y..."

"Well, I'd better leave you guys alone to chat a bit..." my dad said as if there had been enough awkward silence in the room, from his side, "...I have to unload your order from the truck."

After he was gone, I whispered to Cosmos, "Dad doesn't agree with my ambition."

"I know, but we can change that, can't we?" He replied too loud for my comfort.

I looked around the corner to verify that dad could not overhear us, "Change the stubborn Italian? Are you serious?"

"Leave that part to me," Cosmos reassured. "Now, tell me everything you know about aviation, and we'll go from there."

12

Who was this guy? An angel sent from heaven to help a little boy filled with dreams? All I knew was that for the first time, there was a taste of optimism in my flying ambitions.

Over the course of the following months, Cosmos had designed a plan to grow wings on my back, and since the money I was earning could barely purchase one hour of flight instruction in an airplane per month, he had a suggestion.

"Why don't you become a glider pilot first?"

"Glider pilot?"

"Yeah... that's how I did it. It's much cheaper and gives you an excellent foundation to fly powered aircraft."

Skepticism was in order, "I don't know. Shouldn't I save my money to learn in real airplanes?"

"Gliders are more than real airplanes. I am telling you, if you can keep an engineless aircraft in the sky for more than one hour, then airplanes will be a piece of cake. Not to mention that glider hours can be credited to reduce the requirements for airplane hours."

"Seriously?!" He didn't need to say another word. "But gliders seem difficult to learn."

"And your point is?"

The following Saturday, Cosmos showed up in front of my house in a blue-and-white VW bus that looked like it was spruced up for people to go surfing in California: all-weather tires, roof rack, headlights with raining visors, face to face back seats, surround sound and a race car steering wheel.

"Cool ride, dude!" I said as I grabbed my backpack and jumped over the fence. I couldn't spare the three seconds that it would take to open the gate. Mom was trying to follow me in an attempt to give me last minute advice and to speak to Cosmos.

"Thanks for doing this, Cosmos. The kid can barely contain himself. Make sure he behaves."

13

"Mom!" I pouted. But to my mom I would always be a 5-year-old boy.

"Sure," Cosmos nodded and gave her reassurance with his toothpaste ad smile.

As soon as we hit the road we started chatting. After admiring and pointing out the niceties of the van, I asked him, "So, tell me... how did you do it?

"Do what?"

"How did you convince my dad to allow me to go to this remote airport to see you fly?"

"Oh, that? It was easy."

"I bet it wasn't. What did you say to him? The old man is not easily persuaded."

"I just said that I was going to show you how it works."

"Noooo. Seriously?"

He looked at me with the corner of his eyes without taking them off the road; there was that million-dollar smile again.

"I told him the truth. And you know the old saying, 'the truth will set you free.'"

"The truth?" It sounded as if I had sneezed. "What truth?"

"That there's nothing wrong with wanting to be a pilot. I told him that pilots are responsible citizens." He started counting reasons with his fingers, "Pilots don't smoke, we don't drink, we don't do drugs, and we don't get in trouble, well... most of us don't, at least. Because... if we start cultivating bad habits, we risk losing our wings..."

I wanted to interrupt him, but he kept talking, "...still, your dad was not sold on the idea. When I felt his concern about safety, I brought up the statistics that technically prove that flying is the safest means of transportation. Do you know that the odds of dying in a car accident are 1 in 98?"

I shook my head, and before I could voice the obvious follow-up question, he read my mind.

"…compared to the chances of being involved in an air accident, which are 1 in more than 7,000. So, we're in more danger while driving this van." He swerved the VW bus a bit to reinforce his point. I grasped the door handle.

I could see his argument hitting the bullseye in my dad's book of good conduct, principles and safety, but still.

"I also told him that a dark past should not be used as a hindrance to a bright future." He winked, as to say, 'you know what I mean.'

I didn't know what to say. How could I possibly thank this man? I recomposed myself and said, "Thanks… deep from my heart. I am not sure if I'll ever be able to repay you."

"For what?" He laughed as if it was no big deal.

"For giving me wings."

CHAPTER THREE
Soft Water

Cosmos took me to a little airfield located on a farm, on top of a mountain range. To get there, we had to drive 50 miles on a freeway and then 5 miles on a winding dusty road. It was far away from my house; well, everything is far when you're a teenager without a car.

The airport was surrounded by fir trees, planted on what seemed to be an extremely sandy soil; the trees were used for the extraction of a rubberlike resin. The 3,000-foot asphalted runway was oriented east-west, with the west threshold being a couple of dozen feet higher than the east one. Right beside it, to the south side, there was an irregular grass runway, which had the same width but half of the main runway's length. Beyond the green runway, a barbed-wired fence, another line of firs and a 2,800-foot cliff leading to a canopy of tall oak trees.

Looking straight to the east one could see the skyline of Curitiba, the capital of the state. To the northwest of the runway there was a lone wooden hangar that looked as if it was built during the Great Depression. A pair of big rolling doors made of solid wood almost required three nightclub bouncers to push them open. On the sides of the hangar, there were a couple of perfect round holes made on the thick wooden boards where the two slanted roofs intersected. *Why would anyone do that?* I made a note to ask someone about the holes later.

Not far from the hangar, trying to rise above the wall of firs was a windsock pole with horizontal sidebars leading to its top; when the airport was not in use, the new students were in charge of disassembling the enormous windsock (not an easy task if the wind was variable or more than 5 knots). Cosmos told me that the windsock pole was also used to tie students during baptism.

"Baptism?" I looked at him puzzled.

"Yes. After a student pilot flies alone for the very first time, there is a baptism."

"Like... with a priest?" I asked naively.

"No... silly." He half-smiled, "You don't really know what an aviation baptism is?"

"No."

"Well, there are two types of baptisms: glider baptisms and airplane baptisms. The only difference is about the content of what is poured on your head."

"Poured on your head? Like...water?"

"Water? Ha, ha, ha, ha, ha," he laughed out loud as if he had recalled a joke. "After a student pilot's first solo flight, we tie him to the windsock and dump two big buckets of cow manure on his head."

"Gross!" I pouted. "You've got to be kidding!"

"Don't give up aviation yet, boy. In an airplane baptism, we dump two big buckets of old airplane engine oil."

"And why on earth do you tie the victims?"

"Because, after the baptism, the student has the right to chase his flight instructor and give him a big hug. Typically, we don't tie the rope very hard; it just serves to prevent the student from throwing stuff back at you, and gives the flight instructor a head start. In other words, good flight instructors are also great sprinters." He explained, still laughing.

"Well, I'd better start practicing my 100-meter dash, and hope

17

that you are my instructor."

He flashed a broad smile, "You couldn't catch me."

"That's your first mistake."

"What?"

"To assume that I can't do something."

There was a country club, for the city folks, within the farm property called THALIA, written in tall white letters on a wood arch over a rustic entrance. Cosmos explained to me that members of the glider club were also allowed to frequent the country club's restaurant.

It was there that I was introduced to the most active glider pilots, some of whom would become my instructors. They all seem to be expatriates, linked together by a passion for flying. There were several Germans (after all, Germany was the birthplace of Otto Lilienthal - the father of soaring; not to mention that the country has the biggest fleet of gliders in the world); there were also some folks from Switzerland; most of them had heavy accents, but even if one couldn't hear them talking, their looks gave away that they were strangers in a strange land. They were used to gathering in the country club's restaurant, in the morning for flight briefings and at the end of the day for debriefings and cold beers.

Beer? Aren't pilots supposed to not-drink-alcohol? I thought to myself. *Well, looks like that rule doesn't apply to Europeans.*

Pretty soon it became evident that flying gliders was an activity based on teamwork. A person can't simply put a glider in the air by himself. He needs the assistance for others on getting a glider out of the hangar or trailer (some gliders need to be assembled), polishing the glider (dirt and drag walk hand in hand), moving it to the runway threshold, connecting the tow cable to the glider and the tug airplane, holding the wing horizontally for takeoff, being a ground crew (in case the pilot lands somewhere else – other fields) and helping to clean and store the glider after the flight.

That's all I needed, an opening to be part of flying, even if I couldn't leave the ground.

The president of the glider club, who was zealously called "Mr. President," asked me if I had already had an introductory flight.

"Not yet, Sir." I answered with a heavy heart, "This time I've just come along with Cosmo to check out the operations." That was my gracious way to avoid explaining the fact that I was broke. We talked for a while and I told him that I didn't actually live in the capital, like the other students.

"Well, here's a student form and a recommendation letter for your pilot medical exam." He said, handing me the forms. "I normally only give them out after the introductory flight, but since you don't live close by."

With hands aquiver, I grabbed the form and letter.

"Since you are underage, don't forget to ask your parents to sign it."

"Yes... thank you, Sir." I couldn't stop imagining my dad ripping the student form in millions of pieces.

But that heartbreaking thought lasted less than an hour. Once the operation started, my enthusiasm was renewed. The smell of the firs, the sandy soil, the uneven runway, the peculiar variety of gliders silently crossing the sky, the red-white striped Piper Super Cub used as a tug airplane (which everyone amiably referred to as "Jessica"), the foreigners and their Prussian characters, the spirit of cooperation... it all was love at first sight. And I hadn't even left the ground yet.

The seed had been planted; all I needed was monetary water to keep it from drying out.

Cosmos had no plans of going to the glider airport the following weekend, but I had been counting down the days until Saturday. It was a matter of devising a plan on how to get there without a car. I found out that although buses to the capital city ran every half-hour throughout the day, only two shuttle buses (suitably called "drop-drop") were allowed to drop off and pick up passengers on the side of the road. I could get the morning one and the driver would let me off on the side of the intersection that led to the dusty road; from there I could hitchhike or walk the remaining 5 miles. But the biggest problem was on the way back. The only other bus that stopped to pick up passengers at the road intersection was in the evening hours. I was going to get home pretty late.

"Where are you planning to go, Mister?" Mom asked Friday night, as she saw me getting my backpack ready.

"I'm going to the airport!" I said confidently. I didn't say "which" airport.

"Is Cosmo picking you up?"

"Nope... I'm going by bus?" I didn't say which bus either.

"Don't get back late."

I wanted to say, "I'll definitely be *late*!" but instead, I white-lied my way out, "okay."

After three hours comprising of a short walk, small bus, big bus, and long hike, I got to the glider club and spent the day in heaven, helping pilots to get ready for the great thermal conditions that were predicted for the day, and absorbing every detail I could learn.

Except for Cosmos, all pilots that came to the glider club were from the capital of the state (40 miles east of the farm). At the end of the day they offered to give me a ride to the capital, where it would be much easier for me to get a bus back to my city. It would be nice to catch a ride and talk about airplanes with them on my way to the capital, but that would add 80 miles to the trip, not to mention that it would require more money and I would get home even later.

After helping one of the Swiss pilots, he offered to take me to the intersection to catch the bus back home. He stopped at the restaurant to get a soft drink, and I made a collect call to my parents (remember... cell phones were not available at that time), hoping that mom would be the one answering the phone. It was getting late.

"You're... where?"

"Thalia Farm... but I will be home for supper."

"So... let me see if I understand this. You met Cosmos at the local airport and then the two of you drove to the airport farm, right?" My mom assumed.

"Not exactly."

"Did you go by yourself, Junior? By bus?" The tone of her voice was getting dryer as the conversation extended.

"It was no big deal."

"What time will your bus arrive back at the station?"

"I am not sure."

"I am going to send your dad to pick you up at the bus station."

Dad... picking me up? That was certainly not a good option. I thought to myself.

"It is okay, ma... dad's probably busy, and I can walk home."

"What time?" Now all the gentleness had left her voice.

"Six-thirty, maybe seven-ish. It's OK... I'll walk home."

"Give me the right time. I know you thought this through. Do you want to make your dad wait?"

"Seven-fifteen! I wish I could get there earlier but..."

"You can explain that when you get home, young man." And she hung up.

Sirens started blasting in my mind: trouble, trouble, trouble.

Although the timid Swiss pilot talked nonstop during our short trip to the highway intersection, I could only see lips moving and his smile forming from time to time, but my mind was somewhere else, *Dad's going to kill me.*

The bus trip home was slow torture. You know the feeling... when you have to do something that you know is going to hurt, like getting a vaccine, and you start living the painful moment of the shot days before the actual shot (which doesn't last more than a couple of seconds)?

I didn't have to look for dad when the bus turned the corner to enter its platform at the station. It was as if my surroundings were dark and there was a spotlight on him; his back against the car, arms crossed, and his mouth making a colorless inverted rainbow. I knew that the ride home would be an unwanted, anticipated déjà-vu.

I approached the car unperturbed, as if I hadn't done anything wrong. His frowning face just emitted a sigh as he opened the trunk for me to throw my backpack in. We both got in the car quietly; he started the car but didn't put it in gear.

"Why do you do this? Aren't we being good to you? Can't you see that we do everything to steer you and your sister in the right direction?" All of that in only one short breath.

"I didn't mean to be disrespectful, dad. I saw no harm in going to the glider airport by myself."

To make the scenario even more dramatic, a thunderstorm moved over rapidly, using the night as camouflage, revealing itself with a lightning strike that made me jump.

"A teenager boy... going out of town without letting his parents know. You don't see anything wrong with THAT?" My dad said as he accidentally turned the windshield wipers on, full speed.

"Well, when you put it that way..."

"You don't know anything..." And from then on, a cascade of heavy words hit my head harder than the hail falling from the cumulonimbus looming over us.

"... and all because of this stupid flying thing." The volume of his voice matched the thunder outside, "I should not have introduced you to Cosmos."

"No, dad, please. Cosmos has been a gift in my life. I don't know how to thank you for introducing us. He is a good person and you know it. We share the same passion."

A long pause. I was waiting for the second round of hail when he said, "Alrighty then... you're on your own."

"What?"

"Do you want to fly? Be a pilot? Do it... but you will NOT have my support."

I squirmed for a second. *Have I heard him correctly? Did he really say that I could do it?* And, by the way, "support" in dad's dictionary started with a money $ign.

I wanted to jump with happiness, stick my arms up in celebration, open the window and feel the rain, but I knew better than to spit inside the crater of an active volcano. "Thanks, dad," I whispered.

There's a Brazilian saying that goes like this, "Soft water dropping day-by-day, wears the hardest rock away."

CHAPTER FOUR

Needle-less to Say

I had thought that getting my parents to sign the forms, allowing me to take the first steps to become a pilot, would be the hardest part of the process. I was painfully wrong.

During that time, in Brazil, a pilot medical certificate must have been equivalent to an astronaut medical certificate in the United States. The whole process happened in huge military hospitals and took two to three days.

A candidate for a pilot medical certificate had to go through echocardiograms, electroencephalograms, blood & urine tests, vision acuity exams, lung capacity exams, otorhinolaryngology exams, and psychiatric plus psychological evaluations.

The blood and urine tests were very specific and followed a set of guidelines: you had to fast for at least 12 hours and your urine sample had to be your first pee of the day (meaning, you had to have a full bladder). That's when the problems started; the urine test was not scheduled as the first test of the day; so, one would see a lot of guys/girls walking with their legs crossed from one appointment to the next until they were allowed to go to the lab for collection. There was no use in pleading with the nurses to skip the order to get "relieved" earlier. It was a military hospital and they demanded compliance to the rules, even to the ones that didn't make any sense at all.

In line for the eye exam, I overheard a guy begging to go to the bathroom, "Please! Let me do the urine collection now. I don't want to wet my pants in front of everyone."

"You have to hold!" The nurse was indifferent. "What if you have to go while you're flying and there's no toilet?"

Unlike my inpatient comrades, I didn't have a problem holding. I knew that my predicament would begin after the urine sample. I'd never been a fan of horror movies or hospitals, and the reason for that is what they have in common: blood. It's simply not my thing. Being a surgeon was never in the equation when I was growing up.

Even worse than my aversion for the sight of blood, was my apprehension for that thing on the end of a syringe, used to extract it. I was not a fan of needles.

A friend of mine warned me to ask the nurse to draw my blood with me lying down (instead of sitting on a chair like the other pilots). Although it was winter and there was no heater in the place, I was sweating so much that the guy next to me began small talk to calm me down.

"Dude... you're melting. Are you also desperate to go pee?"

"Uh... no, the problem is not holding..." I said, "...I, I just don't like to donate blood."

"Seriously? What are you afraid of? The needle? Or that they will suck all your blood?" He joked.

"I don't like the idea of being poked."

"Ah... the needles, uh?"

I bit the right side of my lower lip and nodded; a tad embarrassed to confess it to a stranger.

The guy seemed to understand my apprehension and was even supportive. Well, that was until my name was called. As I started walking, he couldn't help but bursting in laugher and unveiling my fears to everyone in line.

"This dude wants to fly an airplane but is afraid of a tiny nee-

25

dle." Suddenly, I had become the new joke of the hospital, and the attention shifted from the guy who almost wetted his pants to the guy that was afraid of needles.

"Hey nurse! Get him a lollipop afterward, so he will stop crying," someone back in line teased.

Fear mixed with resentment, I signed my name in two receptacles, took a cup and went to the restroom to collect urine first, giving the stink eye as I passed "my new best friend" waiting in line.

We passed each other again when I was leaving the restroom, with my cup full. The thought of dumping the contents on his head crossed my mind, but then again, I would need to provide another sample.

"Good thing they don't use a needle to collect that, uh?" He remarked with a smirk on his face. "Can you imagine how painful that'd be?"

The next time we saw each other, I was laying on a stretcher, having what seemed to be 10 gallons of blood extracted from my body. He couldn't help himself, "Aaaaawwww... are you okay there, little boy?" His mockery was starting to sting more than the needle. "Did you forget your teddy bear and blankie? I can ask the nurse to give you a pillow to hug."

The cute nurse that was escorting him insinuated a smile for just a brief second, then looked at him and asked, "Do you also need to lay down to have your blood drawn?"

"Meeee? Naaah. That's for babies." He said in his most macho voice."

After my nurse finished "sucking" all my blood, she advised me to stay down for a couple of minutes and then try to stand up little by little. She had been very considerate, and I followed her recommendations to the word.

I finally got up, thanked the caring nurse and avoided eye contact with Mr. Macho as I passed by him. A few second later, as I was leaving the lab, I heard a loud "bump" inside.

I turned around and there he was, Mr. Macho himself had fainted and fallen flat on his face. As the nurses rushed to help him, a pool of blood began forming under him, but it was not coming from his arm.

They motioned for me to leave the room at once, picked him up, and dragged him to a stretcher. His face all bloody.

I learned later that Mr. Macho had to have eight stitches on his chin. Now, I don't wish bad things to anyone, but isn't karma a "fair-bulous" thing?

CHAPTER FIVE

Making Ends Meet

If you have never had gone through a time when you didn't have any money, being broke is a concept that you may not understand. Like hunger, you can only comprehend it when you're truly hungry, and you can only be truly starving when you've gone more than three days without food. Saying, "I'm famished!" when you had a meal 8 hours ago, doesn't represent starvation.

I was juggling three jobs and school to have two flight lessons per month. In an airplane, a flight lesson generally lasts one hour (from the moment the airplane starts moving until the time you shut down its engine). In a glider though, a flight lesson depends on nature; if there are no thermals (or wind pushing up against a mountainside) the flight may last no longer than fifteen minutes (that's the time it takes for the tug plane to take the glider up and the glider to soar down to the ground).

Although I was fulfilling my flying dream, working 180 hours per month to fly sometimes less than 1 hour was taking a toll on me; not to mention that my parents had made it clear that if my grades dropped, I would have to leave one of my jobs and stop flying altogether.

Out of the three jobs I had (delivery boy, linesman and radio advertisement salesperson), the linesman was the one that gave me more pleasure, because it allowed me to be close to airplanes and pilots. Nevertheless, it was the one that had the highest time consumption with the lowest financial return. The commute back and forth the small local airport took me two hours by bus, and my labor remuneration was always uncertain; it wasn't every day that the local pilots needed their airplanes refueled or cleaned. The airport was not strategically situated; their aviation gas was more expensive than other airports, and there weren't many outsiders stopping by for services either.

On the other hand, the advertisement sales position was giving me the highest compensation for the least amount of work. I was not only selling ads but also creating them. On a Monday afternoon, out of the blue, I was summoned to my boss' office.

Oh, oh... what have I done wrong now? The thought crossed my mind as I made my way to see Mr. Jenkins.

The boss' office door was open. I stopped shy of the door and surveyed the place which many people had deemed off-limits. Everything seemed to be made of red wood, maybe to match Mr. Jenkins' ruddy face and light hair. The only things that would not qualify the office as a 'termite's paradise' were a tabletop made of glass and a thick furry white rug.

Mr. Jenkins noticed my reluctant approach and without any kind of formal greeting said, "Come in! Come in... Sit down, Jay."

He's just called me 'Jay?'

We're extremely happy with your performance..." he put the tip of the pen in his mouth and studied my face for a second, "... and we'd like to offer you a permanent position."

I wonder who "we" are.

I didn't know what to say. Part of me was happy for the recognition; the other part shook his head in disdain. You know when, sometimes, in cartoons, the main character becomes hesitant about how to carry on in certain situations, and suddenly two mini characters of himself emerge, perching on his left and right shoulders: one dressed like an angel and the other like a devil? Well, I

29

believe that we have two characters perched on our shoulders all the time. But, unlike the cartoons, it's not a battle between good and evil, it's more like a conflict between your emotional self and rational self, your heart and your brain diverging in opinions, creating a bifurcation on your lifepath. And every decision, no matter how big or small, has a deep influence in what/whom you will become.

"Can I think about it?"

That's not the reaction Mr. Jenkins was expecting, and he almost dropped the pen. "Think about it?" He coughed a fake laugh, "I'm sorry..." He opened a spurious smile, "...I may not have been clear explaining what this promotion entails... your salary will double. And you're going to have benefits... all that good stuff."

"Wow... that's good, Sir. But I'd like to talk to my parents before I sign any contract." I said, buying time.

"Oh... I understand." Now he was swirling his chair left and right, like a radar scope looking for a thunderstorm. "That's a good thing to do, young man. Would you let me know by tomorrow?"

"Yes Sir."

I inched forward anticipating a handshake, but he just winked at me, "You're doing good, son. I see a promising future for you in advertising."

I slid my unshaken hand into my pocket, nodded and left the fancy office with a question mark on one shoulder and an exclamation on the other.

On the three-mile walk home I considered all the possibilities. *What if I am really good at it, like Mr. Jenkins said? What if I get caught in the middle of it and the aviation world gets away from me? What if I accepted the promotion and worked hard for one year, saved enough money for my private pilot's license and then quit? What if... by dedicating my time to advertising I'd have some magical event stolen from my future?*

When I got home, I went straight to my room. I didn't want to talk to my parents about it; I knew what they'd say, and I had made up my mind about my decision. So, the next day, I went to the office and shocked everyone by giving my two-week notice.

You're such a fool! my imaginary rational-self uttered from my right shoulder.

I shrugged him off.

"I want to dedicate myself to aviation full time." I said out loud to assert myself. The emotional-self gave me two thumbs up.

My classmates in high school were getting ready for the un-nerving "vestibular" (a competitive assessment test that was the primary and widespread entrance system used by Brazilian universities to select their students). I wanted to take the vestibular test too, but there was no college in the country that offered the major I was looking for. Hence, I shot to the moon and wrote to the admissions office of a university nicknamed as the "Harvard of the Skies," indicating how much I'd love to be their student.

Six weeks later, their brief and gracious response got back to my hands. The good news: yes, they were interested in having me as a student, and I should contact them back and schedule a visit soon. The bad news: the row of zeros in the six figures projected tuition costs, after a dollar sign. Before I could put the letter down in despondency, I noticed a footnote that was like a final jab on an already heavily hit boxer about to hit the floor; the tuition was <u>doubled</u> for international students. Knockout!

31

CHAPTER SIX

The Perfect Mentor

Two months after quitting the advertisement job, the idea which once seemed like a step toward the right direction, now appeared to be a stupid one. I could not get more work at the local airport and saw my resources dwindling rapidly. Not to mentioned that I was frustrated with my first two glider flights at the farm airport.

The pilot assigned to be my flight instructor wasn't there for the right reasons; he was only instructing because the glider club had a policy which allowed pilots to keep their private gliders in the hangar, as long as they volunteered as flight instructors twice a month. My flight instructor barely gave me a chance to touch the flight controls in my first hour of flight with him. That may cause a student to have uncertainties about his/her own ability to become a pilot, and I also felt my hard-earned money going with the wind.

Why on earth won't he let me try to fly the glider?

It became apparent that the problem was not only with me when I noticed another one of his students complaining to Mr. President. I was almost happy to hear that I was not the only one being literally taken for a ride. Thus, I joined my fellow student in the grumble.

"Sorry guys... that's his personality. I will talk to him, but there's nothing much I can do about it. You know, we don't have many qualified instructors here," the glider club president said.

As luck would have it, the company he worked for, required him to move to another country and no one seemed to be heart-broken by his departure.

Like a prophecy, the glider club became so short of instructors that I could not get someone to fly with me for several weekends in a row. Cosmos had decided to become a crop-duster pilot and had also moved to another city to get his license. It was disappointing to make the trip to the farm and not be able to leave the ground. I was starting to second guess my choices.

Maybe it's not meant to be.

One of the members of the Glider Club was a quiet old European chap that dressed in overalls, and whom everyone referred to as Mr. Aire. Although I had never seen him actually flying, I once overheard a couple of the veteran pilots having a heated argument about flying techniques and finally settling to get the answer from Mr. Aire. To me, he more was a janitor-like figure, a maintenance senior who, when not fixing stuff, liked to socialize over a pint of beer at the end of the day.

I got to the glider club on a beautiful Saturday morning, a few minutes before two other students. The tug pilot was already there, and the hangar doors were wide open.

I was excited to see them and didn't miss a beat, "Who is going to be the flight instructor today?"

Andre, the tug pilot, didn't reflect my excitement, "I have called everyone... no one seems to be available."

The other two students, more senior than me, started naming flight instructors while the tug pilot kept shaking his head.

I couldn't help but venting my frustration, "Oh man. Now, that I have finally been able to save money for another flight lesson, there's no glider ins..."

"I will fly with you." The voice that startled us all came from under an ancient glider that was being restored.

Mr. Aire slid from under it with a shy smile. Not even the tug pilot had noticed that the old man had arrived there before everyone and was working on the glider landing gear.

Does the old mechanic want to fly with me? I bet he doesn't even have an instructor license.

"Uh, no...no worries, Mr. Aire. We do not want to cause any fuss," I stuttered. "Besides, you're busy... fixing stuff."

"Aaah, that's no fuss... I need to clear my mind, anyway." He got up, stretched his arms like a cat after a nap and pulled his overalls up; then, leaned closer to look me in the eye, and with a mocking grin said, "Unless you don't want to fly with me."

"No, no... that's not it... that's ah... you know... we haven't flown together and this is only going to be my third flight."

"Good, I'll straighten you up and make you fly right," he winked at me.

"Uh?"

Before I could argue more, he was getting the wheels in motion.

"Let's get these birds in the air. Do the preflight inspection here and then we can push the glider to 27."

While pushing the double-seat glider all the way to the threshold, I was trying to come up with a polite way to say "Thanks, but no thanks" to the old man. I didn't have money to waste with someone who probably wouldn't let me fly at all. I didn't even know if he knew how to fly himself.

When we got to the threshold, I went to Andre for an escape rope.

"Andre... does the old man know how to fly?"

Andre looked at me as if I had just informed him that Martians had eaten his fluffy poodle. He, then, laughed out loud and got in the tow airplane.

What the heck. I thought.

Without anyone else to turn to for help, I climbed in the front

34

seat of the Blanik L-13, certain that this would be a total waste of time and money.

"Perform the before takeoff checklist in a loud and clear voice, so that I can follow you." Mr. Aire commanded.

I did as I was told, upset for being nice and not voicing my concern. We closed the canopy and he said, "Well... when you are ready, give him a thumb up."

I gave the other student, by my right wing, a thumb up, indicating that we were ready to go. He lifted the wing off the ground with his left hand, leveling it, and rotated his right arm, so that the tug pilot knew we were ready for takeoff. We didn't have radios to communicate with the tug pilot.

The tow airplane went full throttle, and as soon as the glider started moving, with air flowing around the wing, the student balancing the wing let it go. We veered to the left and the left wing started falling to the ground.

Oh boy! My thought came one second before Mr. Aire's voice filled the cockpit.

"What are you doing?"

And I replied, "What are **you** doing?"

His reply was more boorish than expected, "You fool!! You are in control of this thing... straighten the wings up and bring the glider back to the runway centerline."

"What?" I moved the controls and they felt free. My biggest concern was coming true; this guy doesn't know how to fly. I, the student in his third flight, would have to fly the glider.

I struggled but was able to keep the wings level and bring the glider closer to the centerline. We gained more speed and the glider wanted to fly.

"Good... easy on the controls now, and let the glider slightly leave the ground by itself... and maintain it about two feet from the runway to facilitate the tow plane's takeoff.

The man was actually instructing me.

The tow airplane left the ground and we climbed together.

"Excellent," he said. "Remember, this has to be a nice formation flight... put the tow airplane wings on the horizon. Don't be so tense... your shoulders look like clothes hangers. Relax... remember this is a glider, not a B-25 or a tank... you only need your thumb and index finger to fly it. Treat it gently, as you treat your girlfriend."

Relaxing a little bit, I said, "I don't have a girlfriend yet, Sir."

"Why that doesn't surprise me." I heard him laughing in the back seat.

We climbed to two thousand feet with the tow airplane. I was actually flying and he was letting me fly, verbally correcting my shortcomings when they became too horrendous. Not a single time did I feel his hand on the controls, and his voice commands were spot on.

After releasing from the tow plane, we did some maneuvers and were losing altitude rapidly. In less than 5 minutes, we would be landing.

"Make a 120-degree turn to the left... let's point to that cloud over there."

I looked to my left and saw a cloud, far away. "But we're at 800 feet, Sir. Shouldn't we stay close to the runway for landing?"

"Oh... do you want to land right now?"

"We have to, right?"

"We don't have to. We can stay in the air for a full hour, if you want."

"One full hour? But there are no thermals."

"Says who? Turn to the left as I told you."

I made a left turn and headed to the cloud he had pointed out. I was nervous that this guy was testing me and felt I should have stayed closer to the runway.

As we got near to the mini cumulus cloud, my right wing lifted so fast that I gave in and the left wing drop without a fight.

"May I have the controls for a second?" He asked.

Wow! He is really asking me to give him the controls.

I lifted my hands.

"No... fool. Keep your hands on the controls and follow my lead. He turned right with authority. Took the glider under the cloud and all of a sudden, we were hit with an updraft so strong that I sank in my seat.

"Whoa."

He tightened the turn even more and the vertical speed started indicating a gain of five hundred feet per minute, then, six hundred.

I was wrong. This guy can fly.

And fly he could. We gained 5,000 feet in no time. His maneuvers were as smooth as butter, as if he were commanding the controls with his thoughts, rather than his hands. When he gave me the full controls back, everything felt square.

"Pay attention to your yarn. It is telling you that you're flying uncoordinated." There is a yarn string taped on the front top of the canopy that shows your relative movement through the air. It's a primitive instrument that works flawlessly.

"More rudder... hold the turn, don't let the thermal push you out, open it now... this is the core of the lift, and hold your speed."

He is right... what a fool I am. This man is probably the best flight instructor in the entire glider club, and I judged him by his age and appearance.

It was the best flight instruction I had ever had and, unknowing to me, the best I was ever going to have. We did stalls, spins and all kinds of exercises to teach me how to be one with the machine. When we were about to land, because there were other students waiting, I wanted to give him the controls back, but he said it was my flight and my landing.

"But this is only my third flight," I said.

"Well, you will have to learn how to do it sometime. Why not now?"

Under his supervision, I made my first full landing. It was not a work of art, but it was not bad either. When the glider stopped and the left wing dropped to the ground, he congratulated me and kept the debriefing going. I was so excited I could barely hear his words. I knew that someday, if I became a flight instructor, I would try my best to be just like him.

When we pushed the glider back to the threshold, Mr. Aire saw that another flight instructor had arrived. He waved to everyone and went back to the hangar to work in the old glider's landing gear.

Andre came to me and asked how the flight had been.

"Mr. Aire is a great instructor," I said.

"Well, that's the understatement of the century."

"Uh?"

"Joey?" Andre looked at my confusion. "You really don't know who Mr. Aire is?"

"He is a mechanic that happens to be a good instructor?" I said.

"No... Mr. Aire is a legend in aviation... a real-World War II veteran that used to fly Messerschmitt Me-163s (Komets) for Luftwaffe."

My jaw hit the floor hard.

A deeper research revealed that Mr. Aire had been more than an ace. He was a POW, a survivor, a flying gypsy, and an aircraft restaurateur. He was a devoted pioneer who wanted to bring to aviation the perfection it demanded. When asked about his feats, he would change the subject to something more contemporary.

I learned a lot of things that day, mainly that humbleness is the appearance chosen by great humans.

CHAPTER SEVEN

The Farm Airport

There's a special connection between a person and the airplane he/she learns to fly. The same is true about the settings. An airfield is your nest; it's a ramp that catapults you to freedom and an extended hand that welcomes you back to Earth. The little airport on the farm was my beacon, it was my cradle and my fortress; not only the place I got my wings, but also where I met my best friends and fully experienced life (and death).

It is still a mystical place, that almost lost its battle with time, but has overcome changes, tragedies and triumphs, much to the effort of those who prefer to learn and grow with history, rather than repeat its mistakes.

Knocking on wood

In order to save money to fly, instead of going home on Saturday nights and coming back to the airport on Sunday mornings, I used to camp by the farm's runway. Remember, the field was on top of a hill and because of the lack of light pollution, the Milky Way was my ceiling.

But there were some nights when the wind was like a carving knife, cutting through my tent and sleeping bag and flesh, going straight to my bones. In those frigid nights, the members of the glider club didn't mind me sleeping under the wings of the gliders, inside the old wood hangar.

I have never been a fan of horror movies. Why would I go to a movie theater to get frightened? But, when one is a teenager, one can't escape talks about such movies among friends (mainly when they find out you're not into it) and after overhearing conversations about 'Freddy and Jason,' my mind would always play the scene in my head, much worse than it was in the movie theaters.

Hence, during my lonely nights in the old hangar, my mind played all sort of tricks on me, turning shadows into monsters, and every single sound created by nature, made me shiver with fear, which I refused to admit, and blamed it on the cold weather. In my mind though, I could foresee Monday's paper headlines, **"The body of a student pilot is found shred to pieces inside a hangar at Thalia Farm airport."**

Needless to say, I didn't get much sleep on those Saturday nights, inside the old wooden hangar. But the scariest episode happened at the end of the first winter. For some unexplainable reason, when the day was over and everybody left to their comfortable houses in the city, I started feeling abandoned and forlorn. The forecast for Sunday didn't help either: cloudy skies with a chance of drizzle. All of a sudden, a perfect terrifying scenario formed in my head, faster than the rain clouds.

As I lay down under the wing of a glider and on top of my improvised mattress (made of the gliders' bottom seats) the wind picked up, whistling through every crack in the hangar's walls.

Should I have gone home? What if nobody shows up tomorrow?

I covered my head and observed the silhouettes of the static airplanes *staring at me* with strange interest, as if they were trying to read my mind. I finally was able to close my eyes around 02:30 AM.

It was around 06:00 AM when a couple of hard knocks on the

hangar door made me jump so high that I hit my forehead on the bottom of the wing.

The knocks on the door ceased with my loud "Ouch!"

I put my right hand on the growing bump in my forehead, while supporting my body with my left elbow.

"Who's there?" I asked by reflex, without being able to hide the panic in my voice. If there was really a psychopath trying to break in, he would have rubbed his hands in anticipation of easy prey.

I scanned my surroundings for anything that could be used as a weapon. As there was nothing readily available, I got in the closest glider cockpit and unscrewed its 20-inch control stick. It would be my baton.

Good thing I watched 'Rambo' a couple of weeks ago. I thought about the techniques he applied to creep up on his enemies. In other words, I was being naïve and ridiculous.

I looked through one of the cracks in the big sliding doors, seeking the intruder, but there was no sign of anyone outside the door. Then, the hard knocks started again, coming from one of the west-side walls of the hangar, stronger than before.

"Aaaaaaah!" I screamed long and loud, not being able to contain the agony.

Mind you, there were no doors on the sides of the hangar, only walls, and a dozen wings between me and them.

"Who are you?" I shouted at the sidewalls. "What do you want?" As in a bad horror flick, one makes dumb decisions and asks ridiculous questions. What could the person outside possibly reply? 'Oh, I apologize for my manners. I should have introduced myself before scaring you. I am a psychopath and I want to kill you?'

What if he's already inside? The hideous thought just crossed my mind. I crawled to the light master switch and flipped it, as if my life depended on it. The speed of light turned the inside of the

41

hangar brighter than the sun, and I covered my eyes from the glare. *If he is a vampire, zombie or werewolf, this glow will take care of it right away.*

The illumination amplified my dwindling courage and I started walking toward the far west side of the hangar with determination. When I passed by a tool table, I dropped the control stick and grabbed a sledgehammer and a machete.

What if he overpowers you and uses your tools to kill you? My mind creepily suggested. I dropped the machete at once.

Determination gone, I moved as if I was walking on thin ice, being carefully not to make any noise while zigzagging the wings of the gliders. After what seemed to be eternity, I reached the west side of the hangar and gently pressed the left side of my face against the wooden wall, in an attempt to hear if anyone was walking on the loose gravel that surrounded the hangar.

I stayed in that position for about ten minutes, but there seemed to be no movement outside.

Maybe the lights scared him away. I never considered that it could be a 'she.'

I was getting tired of this sinister hide and seek game; well, I was exhausted overall, pure fatigue. How was I going to take a flight lesson, if I survived?

It was already 06:45 AM, the sun was shyly peeking above the horizon. I should be getting up and having breakfast before getting the gliders ready, in case the weather would allow any flights. Instead, I decided to take a quick nap to recover part of the lost night. I turned the artificial lights off and fell heavily asleep hugging the sledgehammer.

Not even an hour had passed when, again, I was abruptly awakened with the hard knocks, now more insistent than ever, KNOCK, KNOCK, KNOCK, KNOCK, KNOCK... short pause, KNOCK, KNOCK, KNOCK, KNOCK!

"Argh!" I didn't care whether or not I was going to die; this had to stop. I ran toward the door and pushed a gap open with my anger alone. There was nobody there, of course, only the chilly wind during the aurora, reminding me why I decided to sleep indoors. While still holding the sledgehammer, I went to the outside corner of the hangar, laid down and peeked around the corner. Nothing.

I was about to get up on my feet when the knocks restarted, KNOCK, KNOCK, KOCK!

It was happening in my face, and I couldn't see anyone. Was it a ghost?

KNOCK, KNOCK, KNOCK, KNOCK!

With my mouth still ajar, eyelids opening up like curtains revealing a stage, my eyes moved up in slow motion and I met the responsible for all the chaos: A woodpecker working his magic on the top of the side walls, making perfect round holes where the tilted roof intersected.

I struggled not to laugh out loud, but started shivering. Not knowing if it was due to relief, hilarity, or the wintry breeze. The woodpecker noticed my presence, turned his head sideways to examine me and after a second or two, deemed me an invader of his privacy and flew away.

The wind helped to clear up the clouds, people showed up at 09:00 AM, remarking that I looked like a zombie.

"What did you do? Partied all night long?"

I didn't do very well in my flying lesson and my landing was even more appalling than the things that had crossed my mind the night before; but I chose to keep the events in the wee hours of the morning between me and the woodpecker. Well, make it among the three of us now.

Baptism 1-0-1
Solo flights were an anticipated occasion not only for the student pilot and his/her instructor, but also for everyone else that participated in the glider club's operation.

There was a mix of tension and expectation in the air because before the first solo flight, the instructor and tug pilot had to create an emergency situation that was far from being just a simulation. Usually, the instructor would disconnect the tow cable shortly after the take-off, as if the tow cable had really broken, with the glider around 200 feet above the ground.

So, all that excitement of "the bird is leaving the nest alone for the first time," had to wait until the student pilot proved that he was able to make a life-or-death decision in a split second: come safely back to the runway or find an off-airport spot to land the glider. Returning to the airport, without stalling the glider during the low turn, was the decision and action the instructors were looking for. If the student pilot completed the emergency without the instructor intervening, that would be the cue that his next flight would be solo.

After the solo flight, the student pilots who had performed their solo more recently (a.k.a. senior student pilots) would tie the new "solo pilot" to a windsock pole (as a payback deed) and the instructor would dump two big buckets of cow manure on top of the poor fella. After that, it was a "run for your life" type of environment, as the student pilot would untie himself and try to catch his instructor (and whoever else he could) and give him a hug. Some people would lock themselves in the hangar, others would climb trees, and some would get in their cars and drive away until the student pilot retired to the bathroom shower. One of the that last methods of escape was the glider club's VW van, used to transport student pilots from the capital city to the farm for flight lessons. After the baptism, the other student pilots would run to the van, cram themselves in it and drive away, until the "dust" settled down.

I happened to become best friends with another student pilot, Jack. Like me, he traveled by bus, from a city by the shore, for his flight lessons once a week. He was also a fast learner and we shared the same views about life. Even when I got to the farm airport early, I always let Jack fly before me, because he could only fly on Saturdays and I wanted him to be able to get a second flight in, if he could.

As his solo day approached, he asked if I was going to dump one of the buckets of manure on his head. I told him that the honors belonged to his flight instructors, but if there was one bucket left, I'd think about the matter (pun intended).

"Are you sure you want to do that? You know I am going to get you!"

The guy had a point; he was much stronger and faster than me.

"Do you have an alternate?" I asked as a joke. An 'alternate' normally meant another airport a pilot had in mind, in case his destination airport became closed (due to weather, traffic, or an emergency). In our case, I meant it as a 'different suggestion.'

"I kind of do." He grinned, "If you are up for it."

He, then, went to tell me details about a plan he had concocted for the occasion. It was simply brilliant, not only would I be spared, but he'd have a chance to catch some senior students that had been teasing him for quite some time.

On the day of his solo, prior to his simulated emergency flight, I went to the VW van and did my part. First, I disconnected the distributor cap; then, I made sure that the back door was left unlocked, and finally, I latched the 'child-proof' locking mechanism of the side doors.

Jack performed his emergency procedures flawlessly and went on to have an even more perfect solo flight. When his glider came to a stop, there were lots of thrilled senior student pilots ready for the ritual and to "run from the bull."

"Are we ready to dump and go? Who has the van keys?" A senior flying student asked.

"I do," I said, showing them the keys.

They tied him up to the windsock and, after two instructors dumped two buckets of fresh manure mixed with water on his head, the senior students took turns dumping a small third one. I dumped a bit of what was left, not to break character.

Jack, then, started to untie himself, vowing that he was going to get all of us.

"Let's get out of here." I said and ran toward the VW van, with six other students trailing me. The instructors had already disappeared from sight. Everyone jumped in, and I got behind the wheel. A hideous Jack, looking like a stinking mud monster, freed himself from the ropes and began making his way toward the van.

"C'mon, Joey. Turn it on. Let's get out of here." The guys started tapping on my back.

"Let him get closer and then we'll make him eat dust," I said.

When Jack was twenty feet away, the students were getting completely insane inside the van, "Gosh, he is getting too close! Are you sure the doors are locked? Let's hit the road... NOW!"

"OK... let's go." I turned the ignition on. Instead of the normal "Vroom," the starter spun a couple of times and nothing.

"Oh my god... what's going on?" Somebody howled. I looked back and there was sheer terror on their faces.

"It's not starting." I tried again, knowing that the result would be the same.

By this time, Jack was smudging the windows of the van with his dirty hands. The scene was straight from a horror movie, it was as if Jack was carrying an electric saw or scythe, and instead of mud, there was blood.

"GOOOO.... GOOOO." They were screaming now.

Suddenly, Jack went to the back of the van and opened the trunk door that gave access to the back seats.

"Who left the back door unlocked?" The students in the rear seats started jumping to the middle seats. The students in the middle seats start trying to open the door frenetically, but since I

46

had latched the child proof unlocking mechanism, only the front side doors could be opened from the inside.

Jack got in, using the back door, and the pandemonium started. He was able to catch four out of the six students that were inside the van, sharing the manure that was all over his body. I and two lucky students were the only ones that escaped without a stain.

Up to this day, it remains a mystery who had loosen the VW distributor's cap, left the back door unlocked and activated the child locking mechanism on the side doors.

Against Boredom

It is said that "Necessity is the mother of invention." Well, if that's so, then "risk" is "necessity's" not-so-famous husband and "failure & success" are invention's twin sons.

What do you get when you have a bunch of teenagers lying around with nothing to do? If you say, "Trouble!" *Ding, ding, ding, ding, ding…* that's the correct answer.

We had a group of what, in the aviation world, is commonly referred to as "Hangar Rats;" a hangar rat is often a teenager so fanatic for aviation that he spends an incredible amount of idle time wandering around the local airport, trying to absorb anything he can that is related to aviation. Our (hangar) rat pack was comprised of a bunch of student pilots and brand-new instructors: Herman (the brains), Sid (the rebellious), Paul & Peter (the trouble twins), Louie (the debonair), Taylor (the rascal), Gil (the maverick), Zolli (the bachelor), Matt (the architect), Wald (the pessimist), Eddie (the naïve), "Wingspan" (the somber), and me (the loony). Someone once called us the "Bad to the Bone Gang," but I beg to differ; we were sharp high schoolers/college kids, aviation apprentices with a purpose.

Thalia farm airport was geographically located in an area

where sudden meteorological changes were as unpredictable as our juvenile actions, and there were those days when the weather (low ceilings, wind, fog or rain) or maintenance caused the operations to come to a complete halt.

Despite any kind of holdup, we (faithful hangar rats) would gather in the airfield to try to burn the fog off (with imaginary laser beams), stop the rain (with seriously pathetic anti-rain dance) or pester the mechanics to finish their work more rapidly.

"Wow... good job, it looks good, it looks really good... I think it's ready... yeah, it looks ready definitely. Put the engine cowling back on and let's test flight this thing!" Yet, there were still parts of the tow airplane spread all over the hangar.

Therefore, in order to pass the time, we would create games that, if there was such a thing as a rating system (like they have for video games nowadays), they would be easily rated as "**K**," for kamikaze.

The first game we created was a much precarious version of parasailing. It all started when I spotted an old deployed parachute on the corner of the hangar, waiting to be folded by a certified skydiver. Since the skydiver, who folded our parachutes, would only come to the farm airport twice a year, the poor thing sat there for months; it was a sheer nylon-and-harnesses mess; a dead giant jellyfish being successful in the art of dust collection.

It was just a matter of using the magical words to get everyone involved.

"Hey, what if we use that parachute and the club VW van to do some parasailing?" I pointed to the lifeless ball of nylons.

"Uh? How?" An intrigued yet uninterested voice asked.

"Simple... someone wears a parachute and we attach a cable to the van and tow him," I said nonchalantly, as if it made complete sense.

"This doesn't make any sense whatsoever!" said Herman.

Ten seconds of silence passed and he concluded, "Let's do

it!" followed by some unidentified chuckles.

"Awesome!" said Sid, "Who's gonna be the guinea pig though?"

"Ah... I don't think they will let us use the van for that," Wald was quick to point out.

You know, in any group of any kind, there is always at least one pessimist; someone that insists that any idea won't work or everything is going to have catastrophic conclusions. Every group must have its Debbie Downer. For us, it was Wald. You would look at him and instantly worry about the outcome of the entire human race. Except that, Wald was a mix of Hardy Har Har and Muttley (cartoon characters created by one of my childhood heroes, Hanna-Barbera), he had both the mischievous, cynical look and the wheezing laughter.

"We can use my car," Sid came with an instant solution, "It is fast and has a moonroof... so we can communicate with the parasailer."

"Is that what they call it? A parasailer?" Someone asked, but no one confirmed it.

Sid was the most foreign of the rats. Tall, blue-eyed, acutely blonde military Ivy League haircut and a mischievous well-cared smile that had REBEL written all over it. Sid's car was not your average sedan either; it was nicknamed "The Flying Santana," because Sid thought of it as the German cousin of "General Lee" (the Dodge Charger used in the TV series "The Dukes of Hazard"). The Flying Santana, an altered navy VW sedan with more power than Sid's brain's cells, had seen its share of wheels spinning in empty air. Despite the history of the car and its driver, we all thought it would be a great idea; well, almost all of us.

"If you use The Flying Santana, the parasailer will soon need a paramedic." Wald was trying to jeopardize our operations with his dark jokes (which only he thought to be funny).

"Bah... don't listen to him; he's just jealous for not being the one coming up with such a brilliant idea." I said, wanting to dissipate the bad vibe before it became a concrete image in my friends' heads.

"Who's going to be the first?" I avoided repeating the word guinea-pig.

There was an awkward murmur among my loyal cohorts.

Eddie had his head down (with his light-colored curly hair, which made him babyish looking), neatly drawing invisible circles on the ground with the tip of his worn-out All-Star camouflage sneakers, so concentrated on his task that his voice got all of us by surprise, "Well..."

Everyone looked at him at once and waited for some valiant volunteering speech.

His pause was stretching too long, longer than my patience could stand.

"Well?!" I prompted, with open hands.

"...it's your idea after all, you know," he finally concluded.

I saw what his comment implied and that everyone in the group agreed with it.

"Yes, I came up with the idea... and I was expecting someone else to be the main performer. We're a team, after all," I said, a bit exasperated, looking around to the group.

But my words just echoed inside the big hangar, finally giving way to crickets on the background (and then, even the crickets became quiet).

"I would do it..." Sid started saying with a smirk, "...if I weren't the driver," He was obviously relieved to have an alibi. Regrettably, for me at least, that opened a Pandora box of opportunities for more alibis.

Matt raised his hands, "Shotgun! I'll be co-driver... the connection between the driver and the parasailer, the car moon roof operator."

"And I'll hold the parachute, preparing it for takeoff," said

Wingspan.

"I'll coordinate the hand signals," Eddie volunteered.

"I'll secure the cables," Herman said.

"I'll take pictures," Zolli said.

"And I'll call the ambulance," concluded Wald.

"Great... what a brood!" I shook my head and snatch the parachute from a wood chair that looked more like a termite condominium.

"Brood?" someone asked.

"Yes... a group of chickens is called a brood..."

Some of the guys chuckled.

"Are you saying that we are a 'brooderhood?'" Wald also enjoyed senseless puns.

"Actually, I am being very disrespectful to chickens. They probably have much more guts than you guys."

The truth was that, deep inside, I was not quite sure if my venture had a good chance of success. Maybe Wald was right, but I would not let him and his sardonic snigger win without a fight. The only problem was that the only one that could end up injured, was me.

I and some of the guys drove the VW van to the threshold of runway 27 to get things ready. Sid and the others stayed briefly behind, in order not to raise any suspicion and make sure that neither Mr. President nor Mr. Aire found out about our plans.

The breeze was stronger than I had previously estimated. I laid the chute down, put the harness on and as I started walking away from it, to straight the lines, the breeze picked up and the thing inflated at once, dragging me back. I planted my feet on the ground, but with one full inflation, the parachute threw me back on my butt, three yards from where I was clinging to the ground. Wingspan ran toward the parachute and pushed it down with both arms, yelling, "Whoaaaaa."

"It's not a horse, Span." I said as Herman helped me to stand up and tied my harness to a 100-foot blue nylon rope.

"Are you sure about this?" Herman asked me in his calm demeanor voice. He was the voice of reason, the chap with the most neurons in the group, a nerdy adventurer. Despite his smarts, he always seemed to be one of the first to get hurt in consequence of our brilliant ideas. He had volunteered to tie the blue rope to my harness just to make sure it would not compress my chest, suffocating me at once.

A drop of sweat left the top of my head, slid on my forehead and used my nose as a ski ramp. I saw it leaving the tip of my nose and diving to the ground in slow motion, just to splash on the runway.

Am I going to be spattering on Mother Earth like that, in a few minutes? I thought.

"Me? Sure? Of course. Maybe. No, definitely not!" I managed to confess to Herman in a whisper. He took his eyes from the harness and arched his brows, staring at my face to see if I was kidding.

Another gust, this time much stronger than the first, picked up the parachute and made it look like the jellyfish was trying to escape, swimming in an ocean of air; its tentacles pulling me without mercy. Since the car was not there yet, the blue rope was loose on the ground, and wasn't for Herman stomping on it, I'd be blown a couple of miles away.

"Wingspan! C'mon!! Bring the chute down and sit on top of it." Herman asked, still keeping his cool.

"I'm trying, I'm trying," said our clumsily tall buddy. Wingspan got his nickname thanks to his stature. His arms were longer than the wings of an albatross, but not bigger than his coyness.

"ZOLLI, lend Span a hand, will you?" Herman shouted to the side of the runway.

Zolli, who used to think of himself as Prince Charming, the peacock of the gang, threw his head to the side to arrange his hair and said, "But I only have two hands and they are both busy." Zolli was sipping on lemonade and holding a camera.

"Now," Herman demanded.

Gil, who had just arrived and was completely oblivious to the whole situation, run to tame the parachute with Wingspan.

By this time, Sid had packed the rest of the gang in the Flying Santana and drove up to the threshold like a nut, arriving with a fish-tail-like spin-out; the fact that none of the occupants were ejected off the car was quite remarkable.

Herman shook his head, "So much for discretion."

I didn't like it a bit. "If you're going to drive like this... FORGEATBOUTIT." I yelled to Sid's elbow, resting on the driver's window. He put his big head out and turned it back to me, flashing a naughty smile that made me very uncomfortable.

Matt stuck his head through the moon roof, "Aah, I knew you were part of the brood-erhood."

Herman hooked the rope to Sid's trailer hitch. My mind began wandering in an insane attempt to run from reality.

Now, if this were a movie, what kind of movie would it be: comedy, drama, action or horror?

The entire world appeared exceptionally dry while I felt an urge to go to the bathroom. Everyone seemed to have a smile on his face, carrying it like a concealed weapon, waiting to approach me and pull the trigger with a 'BANG!' flag uncurling an inch from my head.

Matt got off the car and gathered some of the guys around me. They stood there looking at me.

"What?" I asked.

"Briefing, man, briefing," Matt said. Military lingo for details of an operation that is about to take place.

"Ah, oh yeah, briefing." I came back to reality, "I will give the OK signal to Louie, who is going to let you know that I am ready by rotating his right arm, just like we do with gliders. Tell Sid to start accelerating little by little so that I can run and keep up with the car while I'm on the ground. As the parachute inflates, let's see if I can become airborne. This is just a test run. Tell Sid not to go faster than 10 miles per hour, OK? And when I give you this sign…" I pretended to a cut my throat with my hand, "…tell him to slow down gradually, and not to stop abruptly. I will try to land beside the car. We're going to give it a run not further than half point the runway. We don't want to get attention from the folks working in the hangar. Got it?"

"Got it!" Matt had long bangs that covered his forehead & eyes, like a soft-coated Wheaten Terrier, and no one could ever tell if he really understood things.

"This is so not-going-to-work." Wald had to intervene, "Can I keep your belongings, if you die? You know I always had an eye for your backpack."

"Shut up, Wald."

I saw Matt get in the car and relay the instructions to Sid. I could see Sid's eyes on the rearview mirror, that mischievous smile still on his face.

Too late to back off. I thought to myself.

I looked to the harnesses, turned back and saw Wingspan and Gil holding the parachute like a ghost, ready to haunt the air. Herman was talking to Wald, they were both laughing.

Are they laughing at me?

Eddie noticed me looking toward him and asked if I was ready; I didn't reply right away and he asked again, "READY?!"

I nodded in slow motion.

Herman ordered Wingspan and Gil to lift the parachute canopy at once. I felt a pull as they opened the parachute, a white dove leaving their hands and flying toward freedom.

Eddie rotated his arm and yelled, "GO."

Matt tapped Sid's shoulder and I could hear him revving up

the Flying Santana's engine while holding the parking brake; debris flying my way.

"Son of a gun! Stop it!" I shouted at no avail. I knew that once he released the brakes, the car would viciously drag me. I got ready to run as fast as I could.

I had never seen the entire movie "Rebel with a Cause" but had seen a clip of the Chickie-Run scene, when the guy gets stuck and dies. All of a sudden, the entire situation looked like that scene, with Sid being the cool James Dean, and I was the other guy, the one with the tragic ending. I looked again at Eddie and gave him the 'abort operations' signal. He looked back at me puzzled, and opened his arms as if I just had invented the signal.

"ABORT!" I yelled.

He laughed and shook his head.

Herman saw my panic and ran toward the Flying Santana, waving his arms to get Sid and Matt's attention.

I lowered my eyes to the intricate fastener in my harness and thought that if the Great Houdini could open handcuffs while underwater, in a matter of seconds, I should be able to open the parachute's fastener bef...

The jolt of the car was so hard that my neck almost detached from my body with the whiplash. I was able to do three steps before I realized that the car was already faster than me. It would be a matter of seconds before I kissed the tarmac, thus I grabbed the harnesses hanging for dear life. To my surprise, the ground left my feet, as if someone had pulled a giant pitch-black carpet from under me. I was airborne.

The only parachute/skydiving experience I had was from talking with friends that enjoyed the adrenaline of a free fall. I kind of knew how the parachute controls (harnesses) worked, but had never operated one before.

Another second passed and we were going way too fast, with the parachute still taking me up.

For a couple of seconds, I gained control of the parachute and the world was happy again.

Hey... this is fun.

That thought wedged between sheer terror and rationality.

The next moment, I noticed that we had already passed one third of the runway, "Slow down! Slow down!" I shouted at Matt, who was cheering me through the moonroof.

"Whoo-hoo!"

"Matt... Tell Sid to slow down!"

"WHAAAAT?"

"SLOW DOWN!" I yelled as loud as humanly possible and gave him the cutthroat sign.

The rope was now in a complete vertical stretch and I was way too high and too **fast,** and too **furious** with my friends' inability to follow instructions (okay, I can add another couple of f-words to the setting... but in the intent to keep it clean, let me just say, "too **frightened**").

Suddenly, I heard the screech of the tires and skid marks being made as the car was coming to a complete abrupt stop.

"No, no, no... noooooooooooo!"

At that point, I was riding Inertia's Train to Wreckage Town and continued my forward movement until the rope reminded me that I had reached my stop.

I soared above the car until the rope twisted me back viciously. The parachute became a closing umbrella and gravity did the rest.

With a thud, I hit the tarmac hard enough to rip off my jeans and shoes.

"Dude! That was sick!" "Insane!" "Let's do it again!" Matt and Sid were shouting from the moonroof, but I couldn't hear it because my broken elbow and ankle were speaking louder than them.

Waldo was finally able to fulfill his position by calling the hospital to let them know that a lad, with two broken bones, was coming their way.

More shenanigans

A few months later (after my cast was removed) we found ourselves idle again at the airport, with our only tug airplane on top of three jacks for maintenance. Feeling that our mechanic's patience gauge was in the yellow arc, moving steadily to red, I sprang into action, before he kicked all of us out of the airport perimeters.

My eyes were locked on those industrial dolly carts that were used to move the gliders inside the hangar. I opened my mouth before my brain could bowdlerize my words, "How about a dolly race?"

Sid, who was half asleep inside a Jantar II glider, opened the Plexiglas canopy with one hand while rotating his baseball cap180 degrees with the other.

"Dolly race? Sounds fun...I'm in. Tell me more."

The other "idlers" drew close.

"Simple. We attach ropes to the back of two cars..."

"Oh boy... here we go again. You guys don't ever learn, do you?" Wald, the pessimist on duty, interjected.

"...anyway, we attach ropes to the back of Sid and Zolli's cars and two of us sit on the dollies and hold tight to the ropes. The cars will pull us to a certain point on the runway, just to give us a boost, and then get out of the way while we release the ropes and let inertia take care of the rest. The pilot/dolly that goes farther wins."

"How are we going to have directional control on those things?" said Herman, pointing to one of the dollies' wheels. "The four wheels are independent,"

"You mean, steering left... and right?"

"That's what directional control means, duh."

"We can't! That's the fun part of it," I said.

Wald buried his face in his hands and shook it, "I can't believe I am actually friends with you people," his voice came out exasperatedly muffled.

We took the dollies and the cars up to the now infamously higher threshold 27, and got things set.

"OK... but this time I won't be the guinea pig." I said as I attached a 50-foot blue nylon rope to Zolli's white sport Fiat.

"I'll do it," Sid said, "as long as you drive my car."

"Great! Who else?" I looked for volunteers.

"I think Matt should do it with Sid," suggested Herman.

Matt, who was laying under the back side of the Flying Santana, tying up the rope, tried to conceal himself by pulling his entire body under the car.

His strategy didn't work, as everybody started chanting, "Matt, Matt, Matt, Matt..."

"Alright, alright," he grumbled, "What is the prize for the guinea pig winner?" He asked as he pushed himself under the car.

"Hmm... how does a root beer float sound?" I asked.

"Sounds worth racing for," replied Sid.

"Root beer float and stitches, what a great combination." added Wald.

"Don't listen to gloomy Gus," said Herman.

We had a briefing before the grand race and I explained how it would work in an ideal world. Zolli and I would accelerate slowly up to 30 miles per hour, at one point, I'd signal to him and we both would make a 90-degree turn (I, to the left, and he, to the right) to exit the runway. The racers would then, let go of the rope and let inertia (and the slope) take them as far as they could go until a complete stop. They were not allowed to help push the dollies with their hands. The racer that went the farthest would win.

I positioned the Flying Santana to the left (I'd be towing Sid) and Zolli position his sports Fiat to the right (towing Matt). When the guys were sitting in their respective dollies, Zolli and I revamped the engines, to increase the dramatic atmosphere, and then started driving, keeping an eye on our "wake-dolliers." As everything seemed to run smooth, we accelerate to 30 miles per hour, side by side.

Then, I signaled and started a sharp turn to the side of the runway, and momentum took over our brave riders.

For everybody's complete surprise, it worked!! They passed us and kept going down the runway. Sid won for obvious reasons; besides being heavier than Matt, he tucked himself to make his figure more aerodynamic.

"That was grand!" Sid shouted when I drove to pick him up.

Since there were no victims, everyone wanted to try it, well, almost everyone. Wald was still skeptical.

"My idea, my turn." I claimed, and chose Zolli to be my opponent.

To this day I still believe that it would have worked with us too, hadn't we let Sid and Matt drive. It started as smooth as the first one, with us getting momentum side by side; then 30 mph came and went and we didn't see any signs of the drivers making the turn off the runway. At around 40 miles per hour, sheer terror was stamped all over Zolli's face, reflecting what we both knew was happening: we had been duped.

Sid and Matt kept going faster and faster. The wheels of the dollies were now making a wheezing sound. I released my rope, hoping to regain control. My dolly started veering left and I ended up face-planting on the grass beside the runway. Zolli, though, got the worst of it; having refused to let go of the rope, he ended up rear-ending his own car when Matt could not see him in the rear-view mirror and made a sudden stop. Zolli ended up with a concussion.

One of the instructors witnessed it all happening and, despite our pleas, reported it to Mr. President. We were all suspended from the air club for an entire month, even Wald who had absolutely nothing to do with it.

We were so mad at our snitcher that, a few weeks later, we saw his car at a movie theater parking lot, and planted a dead fish in it (inside the front right-side wheel spoke). We heard that it took days for him to find where the stench was coming from.

Boys will be boys (or rats).

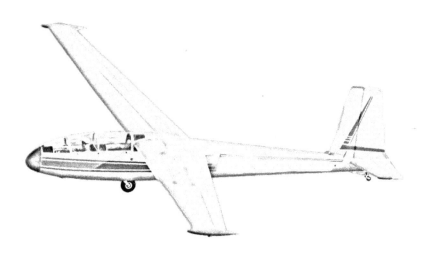

CHAPTER EIGHT
Found in Translation

Movies have this dynamic power to influence our minds by detaching us from reality and turning us into our favorite characters. It's a way of escaping and learning.

My first experience on how movies influence people, happened after watching a rerun of the movie "Rocky" on TV. It was so influential in my middle-school mind, that I even ended up naming my dog "Butkus."

One clear Sunday morning, after watching the movie the previous night, I was resolute to turn my skin-and-bone teenage body into a mass of muscle, just like my boxing hero. I woke up earlier than my parents, tiptoed my way to the kitchen, opened the old white fridge (which had a statue of a penguin on top of it – as most Brazilian fridges had, at the time), retrieved two eggs from the door tray, cracked them open inside a tall glass, vigorously mixed them, drank it in one gulp and went jogging (like Rocky did in the movie).

All that fuss just to throw up my guts four blocks later. I don't recall Rocky on his knees by the sidewalk curb, in the streets of Philadelphia, gagging and vomiting. There was a horrible raw egg aftertaste, and the entire humiliating scene was witnessed by a couple of stray dogs. Even they looked at me with disgusted faces.

"Top Gun" was released when I was reaching the blossom of my adolescence. If you add the factors (hot shot movie) + (easily influenced teenager mind) + (pilot certificate in his hand), it's obvious that the results can't be good. And they weren't. Buzzing towers was just the start. Gil and I did things that would make the flying gypsies of the Great American Flying Circus cringe.

There were only a few of us, hangar rats, that could speak English fluently, and that sort of gave us an edge with girls. I felt like I had superpowers when I became a sudden sensation for being capable of translating romantic melodies in a girl's ears, while slow dancing.

My monolingual friends didn't appreciate having their dates stolen for a slow translation dance.

"It's a low punch that deserves a real punch," said Taylor once.

"What? I am just making good use of my language advantage."

"And I am going to make good use of my size advantage."

"Instead of behaving like a big whining baby, why don't you learn a new language?" I asked him in order to buy time, and cool his hot head.

"Maybe I will."

Three months later, the glider club annual party took place at the farm's hangar. Once a year, the glider club had a ball to celebrate its anniversary and many girls would flock from the country club to our hangar. This particular year, our group was in charge of the decoration and we agreed to adorn it with a vintage style theme, like the Big Band balls that took place in the airfields of England during World War II.

We parked our tow plane and most of the gliders outside, leaving just a few of them forming a semi-circle that was our dance floor. There were placards of war, pinup–girl posters, colorful balloons over our heads, and an aroma of popcorn mixed with burned oil. Someone even drove a Jeep Willys to the occasion. If you walked in without knowing what was going on, you might think that you had just stepped back in time, to the 1940's.

I wanted to play only Glenn Miller songs but the guys thought it would be too boring, so we mixed it with popular songs of the time (the mighty 80's).

I was dancing with a girl who had just danced with Taylor. Our cheeks slightly touching, when all of a sudden, she turned her pretty face away from mine and looked straight at me with her big hazel eyes. I had done nothing wrong (my hands were in a respectful position), but the way she suddenly reacted made me expect a fat slap on my cheek.

The "SLAP!" didn't come. Instead, she asked me, "Joey, why on earth the girl didn't like the bread?"

"Say what?"

"Why didn't the girl like her bread?" she repeated.

"What girl?"

"The girl in the song."

"This song?"

"No silly... the Top Gun song," she said with exasperation as if the song had just been played.

I was even more confused, "Sorry, I am not following you. What do you mean?"

"Well... Taylor translated it to me while we were dancing."

"Oh, he did, uh?"

"Yeah... you know, when she sings, 'Take my <u>bread</u> away?' Is that because she doesn't like bread?"

At that point, I finally understood what was going on and had to fight the urge to roll on the ground laughing.

Should I tell her the truth? After a brief consideration, *definitely not!*

"Well, the story behind the song is that she was on a diet, was avoiding carbohydrates, and... to make things worse, her boyfriend's father was a baker." I said with a straight face.

"Oh!" she was even prettier when she was pensive, "That makes sense. Taylor didn't translate the part about the boyfriend's dad being a baker. What a terrible dilemma."

I was giggling inside, "What else did Taylor translate for you, darling?"

"Hmm... he translated the song from the movie Dirty Dancing."

"Ah... I've had the time of my life." I sang the beginning quietly to her, imagining what Taylor could have possibly screwed up with that one?

"No, not that one...The one about the girl who likes the wind."

Good thing I didn't have any liquid in my mouth, or it would have been a classic spit-take.

"What's wrong? Are you OK?" She asked.

"Yeah... I just swallowed my gum." Lame excuse.

I made a mission to find out what other songs had been butchered by my comrades, and it didn't take long to dig out the victims. Among them, were: Men at Work's song "Who Can It Be Now?" translated as a guy named Kenny, who had multiple personalities, "Who Kenny Be Now?"; Bonnie Tyler's "Total Eclipse of the Heart," being described as a rare lunar occurrence or "A Total Eclipse It's Hard", and, last but not least, Queen's song about the guy who drove too fast, but was worried about wearing his car's brake pads, "I Want to Brake Free."

What can I say? Languages are verbal customs and cushions between nations.

A friend of mine, working as a concierge in an Argentinean hotel, told me once that foreigners often tried to impress him with their Spanish, and would ask questions like:

"Do Argentineans normally put horses on their pizza?"

"I need to have my head cut; do you recommend anyone?"

"Do you have shampoo for my damaged onions?"

Trying to reflect precisely what is being said is like trying to make an international dish without the original ingredients. Translation is already difficult, throw some analogies, slangs and metaphors in the mix and you get a recipe (or "receipt") for disaster.

CHAPTER NINE
The Phenomenon

I don't really know what to call it. All I know is that I lived through it and have never mentioned it to anyone (until now); but its explanation is questionable and that's why I tried to ignore its occurrence. It has haunted me for all these years, but even the word "haunt" doesn't seem to fit... it stayed with me all these years, living at the expense of my own puzzlement.

Due to the lack of funds, I got to a point in my flight instruction when I needed to cut costs to continue flying. One of the ways to reduce costs was to get rid of the flight instructor; in other words, fly solo. That was a good plan, except for the minor fact that I was not ready, not even close to be ready, despite my knowledge and demonstrated self-assurance, which filled my instructors with confidence.

It was my twelfth flight and it had lasted a whole 39 minutes; meaning, I had managed to keep something heavier than air (without any kind of propulsion and without much help of my instructor) for more than half an hour in the sky.

My Swiss instructor had a grin on his face and said, "I know you only fly once or twice a month, but you could highly benefit from a second flight later today."

I was so naïve that I could not see the clues. All I was thinking was about the money to pay the extra flight.

"I guess I could have a second flight... even if it means not flying for the next three weeks."

"Don't worry about the money. I will talk to our treasurer and he will parcel your debt."

It looked like he really wanted me to fly twice that day. Again, if I had been paying attention, it would have been easy to connect the dots.

My second flight was at the end of the day and I dragged my body to get in the glider; there would be no thermals at that time and, financially speaking, it didn't matter whether the flight lasted for 10 minutes or one hour, the flight instruction had a flat rate.

It somehow felt eerie, with everyone smiling at me, including the flight instructor, who got in the cockpit with a big jump, "Ready for this?"

"Yeah... I guess." It's going to be a short flight, anyway. There are no more thermals around," I replied not so enthusiastically.

"It will, indeed," he said. Another cue I failed to grasp.

After the take-off roll, the tow plane, flown by Andre, made a low-bank turn to the right, offsetting the runway heading by thirty degrees.

Geez, aren't we too low for him to start a turn? I thought.

"Where is Andre going? Why is he not maintaining runway heading at this height?" I shook my head.

My flight instructor didn't reply, and in less than 60 seconds, I found out why.

There are two release latches in every two-seat glider used for instruction: one for the instructor and one for the student. They are normally bright yellow, located right in the middle of the panel and used to disconnect the tow rope from the glider to the tow plane. We normally pull it when it's time to disconnect from the tow plane, at a safe altitude, or in case of an **emergency**.

67

At about 200 feet, I saw the release latch been pulled. *'Oh my God,'* it finally dawned on me, this was a simulated emergency (when the instructor releases the cable at low altitude, to simulate a cable breaking down).

I made an immediate left turn, estimated my glide ratio, concluded that we had enough altitude to get back to the airport safely and land in the opposite direction I had just taken off.

After a smooth touchdown, I heard the instructor's calm voice in the back for the first time, "Don't apply the brake. Let it roll to the other threshold."

I was still slow in connecting the facts.

As I got to the threshold, which I had taken off two minutes ago, one of the students grabbed my wing before it fell to the ground and span the glider around, for a new takeoff.

"I believe you're ready for this." The Swiss man said as he jumped out of the glider and started talking four thousand words per second, with his heavy accent.

I nodded at my flight instructor while the *'Ready for what?'* was bouncing in my brain.

"Good, good..." he said. "The glider will feel much lighter without me in the back seat, it will leave the ground sooner on take-off and float longer during landing."

Wait... what? WITHOUT YOU IN THE BACK SEAT?

He kept talking, but at this point I became totally deaf from the outside world sounds. All I could hear was my heart beats echoing in my head and a serious discussion with myself.

Are you out of your mind? Stop this nonsense right now and tell him that you're not ready. Tell him it's not that you are afraid you're not ready. You are afraid and not ready at the same time.

Five seconds of deep breathing and I argued with my reasonable self, *But I need this. I need to solo now. The money is running out and I want to keep flyi...*

"...until it happens. You're a good student, just do as you've learned." The instructor's voice became audible again, adding to the confusion. He closed the Plexiglas and I felt a little woozy. It was almost 90 degrees Fahrenheit outside; it felt tenfold inside.

"You can do this, Joey. You can do this man." I said it loud to reassure myself, but my hands were trembling.

My flight instructor waited by the wingtip, ready to lift the wing and rotate his arm as soon as I would stick my thumb up. For a moment, I even felt a bit pompous about being able to "fool" my instructor; but who was I kidding? It was my life at stake. My hands were still shaking when I finished the before take-off checklist; it was the first time I experienced a shot of adrenaline rush. Despite the fear, I managed to stick my left thumb up.

Oh boy, here we go.

I don't recall much of the flight. I was concentrating so much on doing things right that instead of enjoying it, I was constantly fighting to be ahead of the glider. After releasing from the tow airplane, I stayed above the airfield until it was time to land. As most new glider pilots, I was worried about going beyond the safety cone (an inverted imaginary cone that guarantees that one can reach the airport – the higher you are, the farther you can venture).

Since I wasn't concentrated in finding any thermals, the moment I was dreading the most arrived swiftly: it was time to face the landing.

Thinking conservatively, I decided to start the landing pattern a bit higher than normal. Instead of crossing above the runway at 600 feet, the normal altitude, I did it at 800. Instead of extending the downwind leg, I cut it short. All these actions contributed to me being high on the final approach, way too high, so high that I could have made a 360-degree turn to lose altitude on final, maybe even a 720-degree turn; except that I didn't know that, and didn't do it. It would have taken experience to know that, and that was the least thing I had.

I was high and fast, and I was going to overshoot the runway, that was clear. That thought alone froze my actions. I didn't think, I didn't speak, and I didn't act. There were many options at hand, but none in my mind... from the simplest one, deploying the spoilers; to the more complex ones that were a 360-turn, doing S-turns or a side-slip maneuver. But none of those occurred to me, even though they should have. I had forgotten, in a couple of seconds, everything that the many hours of training had taught me. Heck, at that moment, I even forgot how to breathe. All I had was just a vivid image of a helpless glider, all torn apart after overshooting the runway, and tumbling down the cliff.

Then, out of the blue, my disaster trance was interrupted by the spoiler lever, on the left, lifting and opening by itself at my shoulder level. I looked at my shaking left hand holding the canopy opening latch and got flustered; that hand was supposed to be holding the spoiler lever, not the canopy latch. I looked back, over my left shoulder, waiting to see someone smiling at me, laughing at my shock to find out that there was actually someone else aboard. But there was no one there! All the tiny hair on my neck stuck up. In the midst of the shock, I grabbed the spoiler lever and pull it fully, as a castaway would have grabbed a life buoy in the middle of an ocean storm.

The glider was now sinking fast and the speed decreased... my touchdown point came before the runway midpoint; it was still a long landing, but not so long to overshoot the runway.

I touched down with a light bump and the glider rolled a few hundred yards until I realized I could use the wheel brake. It came to a complete stop four hundred yards from the end of the runway. The left wing gave way to gravity and touched the ground gently. All my limbs were now shaking uncontrollably, but I didn't notice that because I was staring at the spoiler lever. I had closed the lever and taken my hand off by reflex; as if it were ready to discharge an electric shock. I kept my eyes on it, waiting for it to move by itself again. I stayed there, with the canopy closed, until everybody ran to congratulate me on my solo flight.

"Great job, Joey! You didn't have to land this far. Were you trying to evade the baptism?"" I heard my instructor asking, the Plexiglas still closed.

How do you start to physically explain what is physically unexplainable? A spoiler lever has a locking mechanism. It does not have a life of its own; it simply doesn't open by itself.

I have been trying to find a logical explanation since the day it happened, many decades ago. It's still a mystery that is as mystical as life itself.

For what it's worth, I opted to have three more flights with my flight instructors before I allowed myself to fly solo again.

CHAPTER TEN
The Act of Quitting

The contradiction of the title says it all. Quitting is not an act, it's the absence of action. It seems painless, but leaves a numbing sore; you just stop doing, stop trying, no more effort; no more energy to fuel an idea. You can quit something detrimental, like a bad habit (smoking, for instance) or you can quit something wholesome, like an aspiration. Regardless of the provenance of what you are quitting, the effects of its absence will follow you for the rest of your life.

Despite being capable of flying solo, I still was unable to afford a flying routine, like flying three or four times a month, and that affected my moral and confidence. Sometimes, I would go to the farm just to help as a ground crew, and would be embarrassed to disclose the reason why I was not flying that day.

After another weekend without leaving the ground, a fellow friend (Gilbert) caught me counting my miseries at the edge of the cliff by the glider club runway. The crunchy sound of his approaching steps eliminated the element of surprise.

"You're not thinking about jumping, are you?" He stopped by my side and looked down at the sheer cliff of granite.

"Not without a hang glider." I replied without turning to look at him.

"You haven't been yourself since you soloed. What's the matter? You didn't like your baptism? Didn't we put enough manure in the mix?"

I half-laughed, "It took me three days of constant showers to get rid of the smell, butthead."

He looked up at the little puff clouds at the end of what one could call a 'perfect weekend,' and asked nonchalantly, "Why didn't you fly this weekend?"

I shrugged my shoulders, still looking down, "There weren't many thermals." It was a white lie.

"What? I stayed aloft for two- and one-half hours?"

I nodded.

"So... what's the problem, your highness?"

I had to vent to someone, "I am thinking about trying to put my energy in another sector of aviation. Maybe study to be a controller or a mechanic."

"I thought you want to become a professional pilot?" He said, "You know, the glider club old folks say you're good at it."

I tossed a rock off the cliff and we both watched it make an arched trajectory down, and heard it going through the branches of the trees below. I turned to him with a forlorn face, "I don't have a way to make that happen."

"A way?" He made a point of emphasizing the last word.

Being taller than me (most people are), he touched my shoulder so that I turned to look at him. He fixated his eyes on mine as if I owe him a decent explanation.

"Yes... a way... you know... money."

"Ah," I couldn't tell whether that was a disappointed or disinterested response. And then he added. "I didn't know you were also a professional assassin?"

"What?" I scoffed. "What are you talking about?"

"Yes, don't you know? Professional assassins kill for money, and you're talking about killing your dreams because of money..."

I looked at him to see if he was joking, but his face was as serious as an Easter Island statue. I barely knew him, we had met a couple of months before and now, this guy was able to see through my soul.

"Easy for you to say. You come from a wealthy family that supports all your expenses."

"And you believe that you're the first broke student pilot in the history of aviation? There's no rescue for those who bury themselves as victims."

I bitterly said, "Who do you think you are, judging me?"

"Someone who thought he knew you enough to call you 'a friend.'" He continued, "But you know, it's never good to make assumptions, even when the prospects are promising." He, then, put a book on the ground, by my side, and walked away without another word, his job was done.

Whenever we (humans) are put in a corner, we tend to look for excuses to justify an anticipated failure. It happens in school, in sports, at work and at home. If we're convinced that it's never our fault, then we will never be the ones to fix it.

Gil never knew how much that simple talk changed my world. The book (he gave me) had a story of a girl that resembled mine. Like her, I was not a defeatist. I was not going to quit, even if I had to die trying.

From that point on, it seemed that the universe decided to recognize my perseverance with puzzling opportunities.

You can map your entire life, plan it the way you want it to happen, but there are things you cannot predict, like the amusing power of coincidences. All I had to do was to keep my eyes open and a cheerful attitude.

The following weekend, when the Saturday operations were over and everyone had gone to the country club restaurant, as I was setting my tent up, a Beech Baron approached from the east and flew a quiet pattern to land on runway 27. It taxied in and

74

parked not far from where I was setting camp. I went to greet the pilot and his passengers and to introduce myself; after all, nobody likes a stranger camping by your airplane. The pilot asked if I could keep an eye on his airplane while he (and his passengers) spent the night at the country club; they had made the short hop from the capital to the farm for an anniversary celebration that was going to take place in the clubhouse.

I did more than keep an eye on it, I spent two hours cleaning the thing and admiring its design.

Beechcraft engineers have great taste.

I was not expecting it, but when he came back the following day, he gave me enough money for three glider flights, and promised to take me for a spin the next time he landed at the farm airport.

"It is way too much, Sir. You didn't ask me to clean your plane. I did it on a whim."

"Are you kidding? I haven't seen the old' Baron this spiffy since the day I bought it, ten years ago."

He wrote down my (parents) phone number and shared it with other airplane owners that wanted to have their airplane "spiffed." In a few months, I made enough to pay for my entire glider pilot license.

Some call it luck, others, fate. I believe there is a meaning behind everything, an invisible driving force that can't be either predicted or explained. You only see it when you look back in your memories.

Three months after getting my glider pilot license, the shortage of flight instructors hit even harder. At that time, I thought it would not affect me since I was flying solo. But it did, in a deep way.

It was another beautiful end-of-spring Saturday morning, and as I walked the dirt road to the farm airport, I looked back and saw

the enormous cloud of dust produced by a fast-approaching vehi-
cle. It must have been around 50 MPH on a road where 30 were
considered dangerous. It was the glider club's VW van, bringing
5 students and the tow pilot. They came to an abrupt halt, covering me with a cloud of dust. After spitting mud, I got in the van and
greeted everyone, happy for not having to walk the remaining 3
miles to the farm airport.

The first thing I noticed was the absence of a flight instructor.

I asked Andre, who was the handling the 17 ½-steering-wheel
of the van (those VW van steering wheels were the size of a New
York style family pizza), "Who's coming to instruct today?"

He took his eyes off the road and his hands off the wheel as if
to say, "I don't know," and we almost ended up in a deep side
ditch.

"AAAAHHHHH!!!" was the scream in unison.

After fishtailing right and left, he regained control of the beast
and we remained silent all the way to the farm.

When we got there, Mr. President, who we had also amiably
nicknamed Mister Lizard (because his actions were quite similar
to the character in the Dinosaurs series), was already there, getting his own glider ready for flight. He was practicing for the national championships that were going to take place within a
month. Upon our arrival, he also scanned the van for a flight instructor. Not finding one, he became flustered, knowing that he
would have to be in charge of flight instruction for the day, and
wouldn't be able to practice for the nationals.

He, then, saw me taking the dust covers of one of the single-
seat gliders and without skipping a bit said, "Joey! Tell me, have
you flown in the back seat of the Blanik yet?"

The back seat of the instruction glider was only for instructors
or more experienced pilots that could give panoramic rides to
passengers.

"Uh? Nope."

76

"Would you like to?"

"I don't have enough solos yet."

"Not a problem. Let's have a couple of flights together, with you in the back seat, so that I can see how you're doing."

"Uh... I'm sorry, Mister President... I only have funds for one solo flight."

"No, no, no... this is on the house. The glider club will take care of it."

Free flights? Count me in.

We had two flights and although I was totally new to the back seat, I felt even more comfortable than flying in the front one. At the end of the second flight, he turned to me and asked, "How would you like to be a flight instructor?"

I laughed, "Yes... that's the plan... someday."

"Well, someday is today." He opened the cockpit Plexiglas and told me to stay put. I saw him walking to the student pilots and talk to them. There were a lot of nods and he came back to tell me that I was going to instruct the most experience students of the day; but first, I was going to give a panoramic ride to a passenger that wanted to see the farm from the air.

I had planned to become a certified flight instructor, but that plan was down the road, maybe a year away. Being put on the spot like that was part of what I call "the amusing coincidences reminding you that there are external forces that join you to show the way."

I had vowed to myself to be the best flight instructor a person could be, so as to make Mr. President (and mainly Mr. Aire) proud. At the end of the day, the three students who had flown with me, wanted to fly with me again. And that was how my flight instructor career started. In a few months, I got my official glider instructor license and started to get paid (barely) to fly.

I invested every cent saved to get my airplane private pilot license, but that was not enough. Then, a bolt out of the blue

77

struck again. My father, of all people, sold an extra diesel engine he had, and donated one fourth of the proceeds to my pilot cause. "I don't know what got into him." Mom was taken aback too.

I thanked him with a hug, which he accepted uncomfortably, as if I was a bear or a cactus. He had finally made peace with my natural calling, and being used to always being a provider, he was proud to contribute to the cause.

After learning to fly in a glider, adapting to a motorized aircraft was almost effortless. The engine-out emergencies were ludicrous. I remember the instructor bringing the airplane power to idle and saying, "It's an emergency! What are you going to do?" Where most people got flustered, I said, "I'm home now."

Within one year, I went from having no license to having three licenses, and the timing was perfect. Andre, the only official tug pilot in the glider club, received an offer to fly a corporate jet as a copilot. When the glider club could not find someone already qualified to volunteer his time to travel to the farm to tow gliders, they turned to me once again. And, this time, I was ready.

CHAPTER ELEVEN

The Apothecarius Team

Led and inspired by Mr. President, some of the Hangar Rats matured to become excellent glider pilots, and it didn't take long for them to start winning championships.

At that juncture, the NSA (National Soaring Association) was rewarding the three best pilots in the national ranking by lending them one high-performance carbon fiber glider each, so that they could practice and represent the country in international championships. Mr. President had one of the high-performance gliders (called 'Discus'), and our team was completed by two other fiberglass, high performing gliders, and two not-so-high performance wooden gliders.

Even though we had the equipment to compete in the national circuit, we didn't have the funds necessary to pay for all the expenses related to attending the main competitions, which were spread around the country. The only solution was to find a company crazy enough to invest in an activity that most people didn't know existed. And that was reflected by a collection of rejections.

Our sponsor-searching calls were faced with the same question over and over, "What is soaring?"

"It's glider flying."

"And can you tell me who on earth pays attention to glider flying?" CLICK!

We were considering returning the Discus back to the NSA when a local TV reporter decided to do a piece on our achievements. It aired on the 08:00 o'clock news and ended up with the reporter asking Mr. President what we needed to fly even higher.

"Sponsors!"

That got the attention of a couple of companies which saw in the long wings of the gliders and their prominent long trailers, an opportunity to advertise its product on the ground and in the air.

The main sponsor was a perfume company that vowed to cover most of our expenses traveling around the country.

With the new sponsors we felt like rock stars, famous athletes that carried the colors of a fan base (even though the only fans we had were our family and friends).

I was so excited to please our big sponsor that I even had an idea that seemed marvelous at the time, but turned out to be as disastrous as the constant shenanigans we managed to create for ourselves.

"What if we replace the water ballasts in the wing with perfume ballasts?"

"That's brilliant!" The others agreed.

Most high-performance gliders have wings water tanks (water ballasts). In competition, pilots fill up their wing ballast with water in order to increase their weight. That may sound strange because the lighter the glider, the easier to climb in a thermal. However, a higher weight leads to higher speeds during cross country stretches, when the pilot needs to go fast; not to mention that pilots can dump the water in the sky as they complete the final glide and are close to the finish line, which is a spectacle to be seen.

Obviously, the idea of filling up the water bladders with perfume didn't work. Not only was it financially unfeasible (comparing the prices of water and perfume) but also destructive, as we found out (perfume has alcohol, which could damage the water tanks).

Despite our mischiefs, or thanks to them, we became a tight

group of pilots that kept performing better and better.

The success of the team steamed from an unwritten theory in life: **If one person learns something in the most difficult way, all other ways will become easy.** Want an example? Learning to drive. I have always advocated that a student driver should learn to do so by operating something like a 1967 VW Beetle in a place like the streets of San Francisco. Why? Because it embodies the two most important factors with particularly hard challenges, even for the most experienced drivers:

a) The car: for today's standards, an old Beetle is not an easy car to drive: it's underpowered; comes with a stick shift; has no hydraulic steering wheel; and has no sensors or cameras;

b) The location: San Francisco is most definitely not the friendliest place to drive. It's jammed with cars, and drivers are distracted all the time (either by thinking about the excuses they have to come up for being late somewhere, or by playing with their telephones while driving); it has winding roads; it has lots of awfully steep hills; parking is a nightmare; and its freeways are like a war zone.

Same with our glider club. Due to its geographic location and highland, we got used to fighting for every wee lift we could get with gliders that were considered obsolete. Where other pilots would struggle to climb, in weak thermals, we thrived. A positive rate of one foot per second felt like a victory.

Still, our success was a wonder, since the hangar rat essence stayed in our souls, we would almost sabotage each other just for a carefree chuckle.

On one occasion, Matt, Edu, Sid and I found ourselves passing by a rural town in southern Brazil, a day when nobody had been able to complete the race flight, and landed off-field. After retrieving the last of our gliders (meaning... driving to the middle of unmapped farm fields, finding the glider, taking it apart, loading it in the tight trailer, driving back to the airport, unloading the glider and then driving to another unmapped farm to retrieve the next one) we were drained and hungry. As we drove on the only paved street of the one-horse town, Matt stomped on the brakes and the four of us almost hit the windshield.

"What the heck, Matt."

Matt didn't say anything. He simply pointed to a sign that was an oasis for our high and dry stomachs, **PIZZA BUFFET! ALL YOU CAN EAT FOR $10!**

Being far from the main highway (away from big-appetite truck drivers), I bet it never crossed the restaurant owner's mind that four famished glider pilots would be passing by the town with empty-roaring stomachs.

The only, meager, garçon couldn't keep up with our barbarian hunger, and paced back and forth to the kitchen with a new pizza pan, "Does anybody want a slice of pepperoni?"

Edu was the gracious one to express everybody's feelings without grabbing the young lad by his shirt collar.

"Listen... for your own safety, don't ask that question again. Just leave whatever batch of pizza you're bringing on the table and go fetch a new one... we will let you know when we are satisfied. This may take a while."

The curls of the waiter's hair were as big as his eyes, to a point that when he nodded, it looked as if a multi-eyed extraterrestrial creature was accepting the fact he was the hostage of natives in a strange planet.

After we had had ten slices each, without much tête-à-tête, Matt looked at each of us and said, "Okay... this is getting serious now. Listen, whoever eats the highest number of slices, doesn't need pay his part of the bill."

"It is... nly ten ...ucks!" Sid said with a mouth full of Hawaiian pizza. Pineapple slices sliding on the side of his mouth.

"Still... don't we want to see who the pizza champion is?"

"Why does everything have to be a competition?" I buzzed.

"Joey... you're just saying that because you have no chance of winning." Matt countered.

He was absolutely right. I was the smallest member of the group, and knew that I couldn't keep up with them. Still, I accepted the challenge and forced myself to eat 5 more slices than I should; being the first one to throw in the towel, well, in this case, the napkin.

"I knew it." Matt teased, "Boo-Boo Bear has a teeny-weeny stomach."

I had nicknamed Sid 'Yogi Bear,' after the cartoon bear for his shape and appetite. Since we were always together, the others dubbed me 'Boo-Boo.'

To our surprise, Matt, who looked like a lumberjack, gave up after eating half of his twentieth slice. The contest was between Sid and Edu.

The owner of the pizzeria came to talk to us and check if we had been stranded for weeks without food, and also to count his losses.

Sid pushed his plate after the twenty-third slice, "That's it for me."

"That means if Edu eats a bite of the next slice, he will be the pizza champion." Matt said.

"What? A bite? I am not finished yet," Edu said and looked at the astonished waiter, "Are there any pizza flavors we haven't tried yet?"

Edu ate three more slices, wiped his mouth with a napkin and then slapped his belly, "I feel a bit self-conscious, eating after all you guys stopped. I am good."

We were feeling sick just looking at him munching the pizzas.

The waiter let go a sigh of relief.

And then Edu said, "We should stop for ice cream on the way out of town. Is there an ice cream parlor around here?"

The waiter chortled nervously and retreated before Edu could convince him that it was a serious question.

We paid the bill (except Edu) and the owner shut the restaurant door the moment we stepped out.

The "ALL YOU CAN EAT...," sign was taken down, replaced by "CLOSED."

"Ha... it's only a quarter past six. I thought they were open until 09:00 PM?" Edu asked. No one was in the mood to reply. We were so full that we could barely walk, except Edu.

But the best was yet to come... we all agreed that we were way too full to just get in the car and start driving; thus, a stroll would do ourselves good, especially Edu, who was still looking for an ice-cream parlor.

We meandered the half-mile of the main street, briefly stopping in front of a couple of shop windows. No ice cream parlor though.

"Is this the end of town?" Matt remarked in form of a question.

"Hey... why don't we have a race to see who gets to the car first?" Sid suggested.

Of course, nobody wanted that, except Sid himself, who started sprinting right away, still looking back at us to see if there were any takers to his foolish proposition. And then, as he turned, he started shouting, "THE LAST ONE TO THE CAR HAS TO WAX THE GLID... argh."

If I hadn't seen with my own eyes, I would not have believed it happened. A big black beetle had flown straight into his mouth.

Sid fell on the floor, as if a sniper bullet had hit him, and put both of his hands on his neck. The others hadn't seen the beetle bulls-eyeing Sid's mouth.

"What now?" Matt said with little to zero empathy.

I ran to him saying, "Spit it... spit it."

He behaved as if he was suffocating, "I... I, swa..."

Someone said, "Joey... are you actually falling for his theatrics?"

"Guys... he swallowed a giant black beetle."

"Noooo."

"Yes, he did. I swear. I saw it fly into his mouth."

Instead of helping, the others fell on the floor laughing.

"Come on, guys. This may be serious!"

But no one was taking it that way.

Sid started crying between gasps; finally recovering his voice, he managed to say, "I can feel it... hanging on the walls of my esophagus."

The others started laughing even harder. Apparently, the word 'esophagus' had never sounded so funny.

I took the car keys out of Matt's pocket and ran to get the car and the glider trailer. The little town only had an infirmary, so we took Sid back to the main city, where a doctor, who had a hard time suppressing his giggles once we described what had happened, stuck a micro camera in Sid's throat and finally concluded that whatever Sid had ingested, had already made its way to the stomach.

"What is going to happen now?" Sid asked in a puberty-voice, "Are these beetles poisonous?"

"No, they are not," the doctor said. Then, without being able to hold his amusement any longer, he opened a big smile and completed, "The only thing to worry about now is how it is coming out."

We all burst into laughter; well, except Sid, who made us swear to never talk about the subject again.

85

CHAPTER TWELVE

Buds Away

Someone recently asked me, "What was the best flight of your life?"

We all have extraordinary situations that become imprinted in our memory, for good or bad reasons. It's easy to remember the good ones because they come with a pleasant feeling engraved in our memories forever. But there are those that stay with you for noble reasons. That's why the answer comes easily... no need to search the files saved by neurons.

The best flight came as a result of saving my friend's life. It started in a figurative sense of lifesaving, but soon developed to become literal. It happened when he was drowning in a sea of lukewarm affection, and was about to 'tie the knot' with the wrong girl. I threw him an advice-saver and, in total uncertainty, he grabbed it with one hand as I pulled him through the white waters to safety.

How did I know it was the wrong gal? Well, Jube was my best friend and I knew him as deep as I knew myself. I also knew that after a short period of phlegmatic desolation, he would be able to fix his cracked heart, and the overcast days would give way to sunshine.

A few months after the break-up, a series of connected coincidences led him to meet the right girl.

At this point, you must be scratching your head and thinking, *Wait a minute. I thought this book was about flying?*

The flying part started to materialize when I heard the wheels of his car coming to a sudden halt in front of my house. I went to the front window to check out the commotion, and through the threadbare white curtains I saw him skip out of his car and dance his way to my front gate. My pooch came to greet him before I did; when I arrived he was rolling on the ground, while being fiercely licked on the face.

"What's up, Jube? Did you just win the lottery or something?"

"Aah, much better!"

He waited for me to open my hands in anticipation, "Much better?"

"I am going to marry her!"

I stepped back, pretended not to understand his comment and said, "Are you going to marry my dog?"

"Gross... I like your dog, but no."

I squinted, "Are we talking about Arianne here?"

"Yeah!" He said looking at me as if I had just snapped from mental blankness.

"Am I not seeing the big picture? Haven't you two just met?"

"Yes! Thanks to you and your sister."

My incredulous stare prompted him to continue, "I know I couldn't tell when I was with Ms. Wrong. But now I can say that I'm with Ms. Right, soon to be Mrs. Right."

There was no way to deny it. In the few months that the two of them were together, I had never seen him as happy.

I shook my head and looked to the ground, getting courage to ask the follow-up question, "How do you intend to propose."

"That's the spirit," he punched the air with his fist, "I'll need your help, for sure!" Then, he outlined a plan that, although not original, sounded adventurous enough to grab my interest. Jube was going to cascade Arianne with rose petals, dropped from an airplane, during Spring break.

"Wait! Doesn't she spend her vacations at her family's apartment in Camboriu Beach?" I asked suspiciously.

"Yep."

"Hmm... last time I checked, Camboriu **Beach** was on the coast."

"And your point is..."

That's a heck of a long flight for a small airplane." I remarked.

"It's not... Charles Lindbergh flew from New York to Paris with a small airplane, didn't he?

Somehow, that ludicrous comparison was enough to get me hooked, and two weeks later we found ourselves in the farm hangar.

Since I hadn't told anyone about our plan, because I knew it would not be "approved," I had asked him to arrive at the hangar in the evening after everyone had left.

His car was filled with rose stems and big buckets.

"Gosh... did you raid every flower shop in town? How many roses did you get?

"One hundred and forty-four."

"Why 144?"

"They just sold it by the dozen... so, I decided to get a dozen square."

"We will have to peel off the petals of one-hundred and forty-four roses? I asked, fearing his reply.

"One by one," he said, cheerly. His smile was too happy-go-lucky to be considered mischievous.

"Oh man! Remind me, when exactly did I sign up to this?"

"The day you and your sister introduced me to Arianne," he replied.

We spent two hours peeling the petals off the roses; then, I went to my tent to get some sleep, while he slept in his aromatic car, just to wake up before sunrise and peel off more petals.

When the first rays of sun hit the hangar, we had a mountain of rose petals on top of a ping-pong table.

"It's not going to fit inside the airplane." I was feeling dwarfed by the quantity of petals.

I could barely hear Jube's faint words on the other side of the mountain, "It will fit..." he came around with one hand holding his chin and another on his hip, "...after all, who needs to be able to see ahead, right? Remember Charles Lindbergh's airplane? The Spirit of Saint Louis had a full tank in front of him and Lindbergh was not able to see ahead."

"Geez. Can we stop the comparisons between this and Lindy's airplane? The Spirit of St. Louis had a periscope."

"Ah... do we have a periscope?"

"Sure... I am going to get one from the submarine parked behind the hangar, and I'll be right back."

My sarcastic reply didn't bother him.

"What if we don't take all the flowers... just half of them?" I suggested.

"But I want to cause a big impact."

"Dude... if we take this entire load, the only big impact we will make is going to be on the side of a real mountain."

He managed to convince me to take as much as we could, without compromising the safety of the flight. The Piper Super Cub was the perfect airplane for the adventure, because its double-folded doors opened parallel to the relative wind and left a huge gap to dump the flowers.

We traced our route on an old map (no advanced navigation equipment on board) and started loading our tube-and-fabric bird.

We managed to put six plastic buckets filled with petals to the rim inside the airplane: three in the small cargo compartment and the remaining three were stacked in front of him (I removed the control stick off the back seat and we created a wall of buckets between him and me), some between his legs and some on top of his knees. We almost forgot his gargantuan cellular phone (at the time, cell phones were a new technology and looked more like a small brick).

"Are you comfortable there?" I foolishly asked, looking back to a barricade made of colorful plastic containers.

"What do you think?" It was the muffled reply, "Good thing Lindbergh didn't have a girlfriend in Paris, uh?"

When he mentioned that, I remembered seeing black-and-white footage of the Spirit of Saint Louis taking off from Long Island, in the beginning of its non-stop transatlantic flight to Paris. The airplane bounced a couple of times, almost refusing to leave the ground before Lindy finally forced it aloft. The heavy aircraft cleared the obstacles after the end of the runway by a few feet. For a moment, I wondered if we were going to replicate that historic take off. I walked around the Piper Cub one more time for a final inspection. The landing gear bungees (shock absorbers) didn't look exaggeratedly stretched and I tried to lift the tail to have a feeling for the airplane's center of gravity. As soon as I moved the tail, I heard a clash of buckets.

"What on earth are you doing?"

"I am checking if we're tail-heavy or nose-heavy."

"You could have given me a heads up. I ended up with a mouthful of roses."

"Oops... my bad."

"It's clear that we are not nose-heavy..." He stuck his face out of the side window, "...we're rose-heavy."

His attempt of joke was so lame that I almost dropped the tail, "Wow... love does make people more pathetic than they are."

I carefully lowered the tail to the ground and walked back to the cockpit, pushed the mixture full rich, turned the magnetos on, asked Jube to push on the brakes with his feet and hold the throttle back (to idle), took the chocks off the wheels (threw them to the side because there wasn't enough space to take them) and got ready to hand-prop the propeller.

"Don't tell me this thing doesn't have a starter." I heard Jube saying.

"Well, this 'thing' is going to make your proposal memorable... I went around to the nose of the aircraft and shouted, CONTACT!" as I swung the prop downwards, praying for the barnstorm gods to make the engine start. The old Super Cub engine was famous for its unwillingness to start in the morning, like a teenager that doesn't want to get out of bed to go to school.

It was our lucky day; the engine sputtered once, twice, coughed some smoke and then fired up all cylinders. I climbing on board and closed the door as fast as I could to avoid the idle engine draft blowing the precious petals. The bumpy serpentine taxiing didn't make Jube's juggling job any easier (taildraggers - airplanes with a tail wheel instead of a nose wheel – have to be taxied in an "S" pattern (zigzagging), so that the pilot can check the sides to have a view of what's in front of him).

"Are we there yet?" He shouted behind the flowers.

After my before-takeoff checks I asked him, "Are you ready for this?"

"If by 'ready' you mean, not suffocated by hundreds of petals of roses yet? Yes, I am."

It wasn't as dramatic as the Spirit of Saint Louis takeoff; the flowers didn't weigh much; the only nuisance was that, with the side air vents opened, they started flying all over the cockpit, and we had to close the vents and endure the heat. Yes, you guessed it... no A/C either.

The flight over the countryside was beautiful, with us flying only 2,000 feet above the ground, changing altitude only when the topography demanded. Every now and then, Jube would open his window (losing a bunch of flowers) stick his head out and scream "WEE, WEE, WEE," as loud as he could, the words being carried by the wind.

We flew over prairies and mountains, waterfalls and rain for-est, finally reaching the Atlantic Ocean and following its white sand beaches southbound. As we passed a busy port, we caught sight of the white concrete runway of an airfield called Navigators, an airport with a control tower and fuel, and less than 20 minutes from our final target.

We landed at Navigators, as planned, to refuel and to revise our plot. The lad that came to fuel the airplane was dazed, "Where are you guys heading with so many flowers? A wedding?"

"We are going to do something that hopefully will lead to a wedding," Jube replied.

We rehearsed our plan one last time: two minutes prior to our arrival over the building, where Arianne was staying, I would give Jube a thumbs up, meaning that it was time for him to call her (with his huge cell phone) and ask her to come to the balcony of her apartment (which was located on the very top floor). Then, I'd make some tight circles over the balcony while he would open the airplane window and cascade the flowers over her, while popping the question. It was a nice plan, on paper at least.

Back in the air, it didn't take long for us to spot the target and Jube's anxiousness started to build up, "Should I call her now?" He shouted

"NO, not yet."

A few minutes passed, "How about now?"

I shook my head once more.

When I finally gave him the thumbs up, he dialed her number and moved his brick-size phone to his right ear.

"It's ringing," he said in a shaky voice.

Before the flight, we had considered the possibility of Arianne being out and about. Jube told me that he had asked Arianne's mom for help with the plan, to keep her in the apartment at noon. He also asked Arianne to stay in the apartment because he was going to call her at noon (she didn't have a cell phone). Now, we were almost 30 minutes late. What if she had got tired of waiting?

"Nobody's answering..."

Oh boy, I thought while we were about to start the first circle over her building, *all this trouble for n...*

"Hello! Arianne?" a brief pause and he was all excitement again, "Go to the balcony... why? Go and you'll see why. I will call you right back."

I spotted her opening the glass door and stepping out into the balcony, holding a cordless phone. I rolled my wings over the building and shouted over the engine noise, "Bombs away" (like they do in the WWII movies).

"What? Bombs away?" He asked, confused.

"Petals away, flowers away." I was struggling to keep the wingtip pointed to her.

He opened the double-folded door and unloaded the first bucket of flowers, but it fell far away from the balcony.

Even so, I could see the smile in her face, as she recognized the occupants of the tiny airplane flying overhead.

"Closer, closer." Jube shouted, "The flowers are falling away from the balcony."

"I don't know if I can get any closer." I replied, "We are already closer than we should be."

"Really? It seems so far to me."

Although I could not see his face, I felt the weight of disappointment in his voice, and I said, "OK... get ready for the next bucket, I am going to tighten the circle and get closer."

"ATTABOY."

I dropped the wing and increased the power to maintain a high speed (and avoid a stall), got really close to the building and said, "Buds away!"

This time we hit the bull's-eye; Arianne had her arms open to the sky and the biggest and brightest grin in the world, enjoying every petal that floated down to her face. It's something I'll never ever forget.

After four buckets of roses had been dumped, Jube called her again. We were so close that I could see her pressing the "talk" key on the phone.

"WILL YOU MARRY ME?" I heard him asking out loud on the phone, trying to triumph over the airplane noise and wind.

One didn't have to be a lip reader to see the little word leaving her mouth, followed by many nods.

"She said 'yes,' she said 'yes.' He patted my head stronger than I'd have preferred.

Then he proceeded to cascade her with the two remaining buckets.

People were on their balconies, in the building and all the adjacent buildings; some were clapping, others were waving and there were some that were making fists and obscene gestures. An old, hairy chested guy, wearing checkered boxers was pointing at us and saying words that I was glad I couldn't hear. That's when I thought that I might get in trouble.

I turned back to Jube, all the buckets emptied and stored behind the back seat, and said, "We have to get out of here!"

This time he lifted his thumb and closed the doors, "Mission completed."

He called her one more time as I pointed the plane away from the building and climbed as fast as I could.

The flight back was even merrier that the flight in. When we got back, Jube called her one more time and was told that Arianne's mom was on the street when we dumped the first load of flowers and missed the building. People, on the sidewalk, put their hands up to the falling petals, and were smiling as her mom tried to explain to everyone that those flowers were for her daughter.

A couple of weeks later, two envelopes arrived by mail, on the same day. The first envelope contained a notice informing me that someone had filed a formal complaint about an airplane flying too low and too close to a building, dropping flowers all over it. Keep in mind, this all happened way before the year 2001. Still, I had some serious explaining to do to the aviation authorities.

The second envelope contained a much merrier announcement. A simple, yet elegant white invitation with embossed letters and ribbons, inviting me to a wedding ceremony of two loving souls who wanted to share the special occasion with their favorite pilot friend.

The contents of the second envelope made the first one worthwhile.

As a poet once wrote, "May it be eternal while it lasts."

CHAPTER THIRTEEN

Aviligion

A few months after I became a tow pilot, one of the aircraft owners, whose airplane I always kept spotless, casually told me that there was a new glider club opening about 210 miles from my hometown.

"So, Joey… I heard from a friend that they have just established a glider club in his town. They got a brand spanking new instruction glider and a used single-seat one."

"That's nice." I said nonchalantly, while cleaning his airplane. "But they will also need a tow plane?"

"My friend is going to lend them his Piper Super Cub until they can get their own."

I was listening to him while buffing the top of the right wing.

He continued, "I also heard that they are looking for someone who is a proficient flight instructor and tug pilot."

I stopped my 'wax on and wax off' movement on the spot and glared at him without saying a word.

"I know I'm going to regret this, because my Skylane will never be this shiny again." There was a short pause, now it was too late to withdraw the thought, "But… I told him about you and he asked me to ask if you would be interested in traveling to the city of Mourao Field to be their first flight instructor?"

I said "yes" even before I could figure out when or where

Mourao Field was located.

Five days and a few phone calls after our conversation, I hopped on a bus, carrying two borrowed parachutes with me (a requirement for flight instruction in gliders) and endured the 6-hour bus ride, which would become a weekend ritual, to Mourao Field. The beginning of a new chapter in my life.

I had never met a bunch of people more enthusiastic about aviation than the Mouraoenses. They had an almost-hillbilly way of chatting and a certain gullibility that could not be found in big city folks.

Having an air club in the city was more a necessity than just a sign of pride. At the time, the nearest flight school was almost three hours away.

When I got to the city for the first time, I felt like an aviation pioneer turned into celebrity. I had the powers that they desired, and was willing to share those powers. It was as if flying was a potent drug, which they became highly addicted. Aviation was turned into a cult, a new religion: Aviligion.

I used to arrive at the city's bus station around 05:00 on Saturday mornings, and a different student would pick me up every time and take to his house, where I would take a 2-hour nap (after failed attempts to sleep during the bumpy bus ride). By 09:00 o'clock everyone was ready to fly.

Twelve flights later, I would check in a hotel, take a shower and meet with them again in a restaurant, where the informal debriefing would take place. On Sunday mornings, I'd give them ground school classes from 08:00 to noon and then more flying until I had to catch a bus back to my hometown.

Since the sequence of flights was 'first come, first served,' as soon as ground school ended, a total chaos materialized; with students jumping in their cars and driving to the airport (3 miles away) like maniacs. I had to put an end into that practice before someone got killed or seriously hurt, and changed the order of who was going to fly first in accordance to their performances in my written tests.

These long weekends lasted for 6 months, until the glider club, satisfied with the results, offered me a permanent position and I moved to Mourao Field.

There were lots of riveting peculiarities about the farming city. The soil was bright red, to a point that at the end of the day, the collar of my white pilot shirt had a distinct red line. The city's airport runway was in a weird location. The single paved runway was boxed in the middle of a strange development: to its west side, a main highway ran parallel to the runway; on the east side, there was an underprivileged housing complex with unpaved streets, and a cemetery on the south side. Only the north side had a clear escape route, in case someone overshot the runway. When I first saw it from the air, flying with one of the glider club founders, I couldn't help but noticing a wide red stripe right on its middle, crossing the asphalted pavement.

"What's with the red stripe on the middle of the runway?"

"It's a track!" He said, as if that explained everything.

"A track?"

"Yes, marks from foot traffic. You see, the runway was already there when they built that development on the east. There is a rumor that a politician had promised to build a walkway above the airport runway."

"You're kidding."

"We both know that's not plausible, but the people living in the development didn't. Of course, the walkway was never built. And since our soil is red and people walk across the runway to reach the bus stop located by the highway, the red stripe was inevitable."

He told the story as if it was one of the matters of life that it is what it is.

98

"People cross the runway on foot?"

"Yeah. So, better watch out for pedestrians when you are on final."

"Watch out for pedestrians?" I was having a hard time accepting the facts. "We're in a glider, for goodness' sakes. What are we supposed to do? Install a horn in the glider and blow it on final?"

"Not a bad idea." He said, missing my mockery.

"How about putting a fence along the airport perimeter?"

"Don't you think we have already tried that? They cut the wires all the time. But don't worry, most people look both ways before crossing."

I couldn't believe what I was hearing.

That became a problem on the day my first student soloed.

Being in 'attention mode,' I saw when an old lady with a hunched back approached the edge of the runway and stopped for a second. I saw her head turning toward the final approach and that gave me some relief.

She won't cross.

As soon as I made that assumption, she started crossing.

"NO, NO!! OUT! OUT! AIRCRAFT ON FINAL! GET OFF OF THE RUNWAY.

The student touched down briefly, but had enough speed (and reaction) to close the spoilers and get the glider airborne for two seconds. It lifted sufficiently to miss the lady's head, who fell on her butt, startled by the shadow and movement of the glider above her. The second touchdown was not pretty, as the glider stalled about one foot above the tarmac; nevertheless, everybody survived without a scratch.

I ran to check on the lady.

"Are you okay?" I asked, helping her to stand back on her feet.

She didn't have a single tooth. She looked at me with nebulous eyes, and squeezed my hands to show gratitude. Even if it

99

had been a B-17 landing, she would not have seen or heard it. She was half blind, and completely deaf.

Following that almost-tragic episode, I had an appointment in the mayor's office and demanded the construction of a concrete wall between the village and the runway, just to be told by the city treasurer that the municipality didn't have funds set aside for such projects. I was almost kicked out of the office when I suggested that they should use the money destined for the promised walk-way above the runway. Tired of my demands, the mayor finally sent a crew to rewire the fence. It was cut open less than two days later.

To say that my first batch of students were sharp is an under-statement. They kept an "A" average in my most difficult tests about regulations, meteorology, principles of aerodynamics, navigation and aircraft maintenance. When the final official test came, they aced it, and the air club got the highest marks in the country. They were even sharper at flying, learning fast and applying the theory to procedures without my intervention.

It was not so much that they had a condescending attitude, but rather confidence in everything that they learned from me. One of these students was nicknamed "Marmot" (six letters that were part of his last name). He was one of those aviation walking-encyclopedias that one finds in the business every now and then. There was no airplane in the sky that he couldn't name or spit out the specifications with his eyes closed. Marmot was one of the top students in the class and one of the first to be ready to fly solo. His confidence was so unshakable that I decided to do some the-atrics during his emergency flight, just to check his reaction.

Every glider has an emergency latch that detaches the cockpit Plexiglas from the fuselage. If necessary, one can pull the latch and due to relative wind, the thing flies away and one can bail out and use the emergency parachute. It's the closest thing to an ejector seat. In all my years flying gliders, I had only seen it used twice, in championship regattas, where gliders fly close to each other and the danger of midair collisions increase.

My plan was to create some chaos during the emergency flight to see if Marmot would be bothered and lose his concentration.

I knew he knew the simulated emergency flight was coming as soon as the tow plane flew a diagonal pattern after takeoff; he even dared to joke about it, "Hmm, I wonder why he is not flying runway heading."

Smarty pants, I will show what overconfidence can do to you.

At 600 feet I disconnected the cable and created the biggest commotion in the cockpit, yelling, "Oh my God, we're going to die, I am going to bail out!"

He made a text-book left turn without wasting speed or altitude. I could even hear him laughing at my terrible acting. That irritated me a little bit, and I decided to push the theatricals a little further. As we were passing over the cemetery, very low, I pulled the latch, pretending to eject the cockpit. My idea was to just pull the latch with my right hand, but hold the thing with my left hand.

Well, it didn't work that way. When I pulled the latch, it opened a small crack in the front part of the cockpit top, enough for the wind to catch and lift it hard. I tried to hold on to it, but the entire cockpit top went flying.

"What the heck are you doing?" Marmot shouted over the wind noise. We were flying a convertible glider.

The Plexiglass cover tumbled down toward the cemetery, hit a tomb and disintegrated in a million pieces, only its skeleton remained (pun intended).

As we were touching down, Marmot was laughing and crying at the same time.

"What a foolish* instructor you are! Now I won't be able to solo today. (*he actually used a different adjective).

That was true, he was not able to solo that day. I had to go to the cemetery to retrieve the metal structure of the canopy and get in a bus to travel to the factory to order a new one which, by the way, was discounted from my salary.

Marmot flew solo the following weekend, when the old lady crossed the runway.

As time passed, it was apparent that I was a good fit to the city aviation scene, and other aircraft owners started hiring me as their part-time personal pilot. That's how I attained my commercial pilot license, multi-engine and IFR certificates.

Things were looking good until one day, when the Baron owner that had referred me to the Aeroclub, asked them if he could 'borrow' me for a weekend. He needed a trustworthy pilot to fly members of his family from the capital to another city. They said no, and I was the last one to know.

"How come?" I asked the glider club president.

"The flight would take you for four days. You would have to get on a bus, travel to the capital, fly his family back and forth and then, get on a bus back here. We assumed that you wouldn't want to do that... and besides, weekends are our busiest time."

I started having this uneasy feeling that they saw me as their possession. You know, when someone behaves like a jailer, you start feeling like a prisoner.

After two years as a flight instructor, it was as if I were marking time, as if I could simply keep doing what I was doing for the rest of my days on earth. In fact, for having one the best approval rates in the country, I got invited to attend an advanced flight instructor course completely paid for by the government. Not only that, but the civil aviation agency was also going to donate a brand-new aircraft to the glider club, which now was elevated to an air club category.

To everyone's shock, myself included, I declined the invitation for the advance instructor class. It started to look like every time life presented me safe choices, I ran away from it.

It is said that we are so interrelated that not a single tree falls or another human being is left to suffer without each of us being impacted, in one way or another. İt is said that every current change, no matter how insignificant it may seem, snowballs to become a big change in your future.

What happens when you reach those pivot points in life, a time when the road bifurcates and you have to choose between two diverse predestines. What happen to the "you" that chooses to go to the right, when you choose to go to the left?

I chose to go left. Little did I know that a dam of regret had already broken along that way.

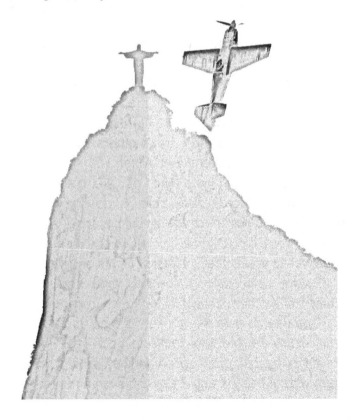

CHAPTER FOURTEEN

It's a Jungle Out There

I've always daydreamed about going to exotic places in the world: Ayers Rock, Horseshoe Canyon, Canary Islands, Koh Rong Samloem, Madagascar, Easter Island, Hoi An and the Amazon Forest, to name a few.

One of the student pilots, in Mourao Field, had three brothers who were skillful pilots flying in the Amazon. The family had an air taxi in the western side of the state of Acre, by the Peruvian border. Every now and then, the brothers would make a trip to the south to visit their parents and sister.

Teaching Layla was a piece of cake. It seemed that her entire family had aviation in their blood and flying came naturally. The brothers could not teach the sister because, as it goes with most siblings, they didn't know how to communicate constructive criticism well to each other, and their flights always ended with fights.

Before I came along, she had vowed not to fly anymore because her brothers expected too much from her.

One day, to give me a token of their appreciation for teaching their sister, the brothers took me up in their exotic Cessna 195 (which once belonged to an airline). That's when I pummeled them with questions about flying in such a remote area.

During one of these visits, noticing my interest, the oldest brother said, "Why don't you come to the Amazon to fly with us?"

"How serious are you?" I asked.

"How serious are **you**?" He returned the question.

He didn't have to ask that question twice.

There was only one major problem. In order to fly in the Amazon, pilots had to take a series of vaccines (malaria, dengue, typhoid fever, etc.). And shots, they meant needles!

"Hello, nurse. I'm here to take the shots required for pilots going to fly in the Amazon."

"Enter that room and pull both your sleeves up to your shoulders, I'll be there in a second."

Short stature, wide shoulders, uncombed hair pointing different directions, with the corners of her lips pointing down, that nurse looked grim. A wannabe witch who failed the mixed potions test.

"Argh... how big are the needles?"

"What?"

"The needles... how big are they? I'm not much a fan."

She stopped what she was doing and looked me in the eye, "You gotta be kidding me. You are a pilot...going to fly in one of the most dangerous places in the world ... and you are afraid of needles? Give me a break."

I slowly looked the other way, like a guilty dog that wet the sofa due to fireworks.

"There are no needles." She finally said.

"Wait... what? Are the vaccines taken orally?"

"No, of course not. We use a jet injector."

She saw the question mark on my face and said in one single breath, "It's an inoculating nozzle that uses a high-pressure narrow jet for injecting liquid instead of a hypodermic needle that penetrate the epidermis."

"Oh... wow, great." I said, pretending to understand what I heard.

That means it won't hurt. I naively thought.

The first shot felt like a saber blade penetrated my arm.

"Ouch! That really hurts. You said it wouldn't hurt.

"No, I said that we don't use needles. That's completely different."

She got a different jet gun, smaller than the first one.

"Is the second one going to hurt as much?"

"I can't promise anything."

The second one hurt even more. Now, there are ways and ways to deal with a jet injector. The nurse was handling it as if I were stock in a corral.

For the last one, she put me sideways, against the wall, pressed the jet injector hard on my arm and fired away. It felt as if the liquid was a missile that had entered my arm and exploding into a million pieces of flak.

I had a feeling she was some kind of sadomasochist because she could not hide her enjoyment with my pain.

"You're done." She continued, "Go home and rest. I wouldn't do anything in the next 24 hours. You will have a fever with chills, and your arm will be so painful, you will want to detach it from your body."

Now, I bet she is just messing up with me.

She filled out the paperwork and started talking about how much she wanted to fly. She had only flown twice and liked it very much. She kept talking, oblivious to the pain I was already feeling.

I collected the paperwork (proof that I had had the shots), got on a bus, barely made it home and thought that death was on its way. The fever and pain were so violent that I had to be taken to the E.R. for observation.

I'm not a vindictive person, but one week later, when I became human again, and after talking to a couple of other pilots who had been a victim of the same nurse, I went back and offered to take her for a sightseeing flight.

She remembered me, "Look who is back... the 'lion-pilot.'"

"Lion-pilot?"

"Yes," she said laughing, "have you never seen the Wizard of Oz?"

"Oh." I said, understanding where she was going with that, "Anyway... I am here to invite you for an airplane ride."

"Really? Why?" She asked suspiciously.

"Well, you had mentioned you flew twice and liked it, and since you took care of me last week..."

"I don't have money to pay for the flight."

"It's my treat," I said with my sweetest voice, "Whenever you can, in the next couple of days."

She studied my expression for a moment, checking if I was bluffing.

"How about the day after tomorrow?" She asked, still suspicious, "It's my day-off."

"It's a date."

She totally fell in my trap. I borrowed a Cessna Aerobat from a friend and gave the nurse the wildest ride of her life, with all the aerobatic maneuvers the little airplane could stand. She screamed, like a dying pig, during the first stall, followed by a three-turn spin (probably because I acted as if I had completely lost control of the aircraft). Then, I performed some back-to-back loops, some rolls, and you could stick a fork in her, she was done!

When we arrived back to the local FBO, she got out of the airplane as soon as I pulled the mixture lever out, and headed straight to the ladies' room, spending almost 20 minutes there. Then, she emerged with a big stain on her shirt, passing by a bunch of pilots who had been prey to her injection gun harshness.

One of the pilots asked her with a grin that could not be concealed, "Not feeling very good today nurse, are you?"

She stormed off the airport premises ferociously. We learned that she quit her job at the clinic the following day. And I felt like an aviation hero. My actions were going to preclude many pilots from suffering in her hands.

Two weeks later, I was on a commercial flight to the heart of the Amazon. The one-way airplane ticket and the accommodations for the first week drained my savings account, again.

You know when you have high expectations about a destination, mainly on vacations, and when you finally get there, it turns out to be a bust?

It started as soon as the flight attendant opened the door of the 737-200. The heat and humidity were so intense that I thought there was a guy with a flamethrower, greeting people at the door. There was no other way to describe the heat but calling it 'oppressive;' a glare shield created by the locals to avoid alien invasion.

I went straight to the air taxi office, looking for the brothers, but they were out, flying. The two people in the office looked at me as if I were a curiously unorthodox human specimen with overwhelmed perspiration glands. Since the brothers were not there, and nobody knew when my assignment would begin, I got in a cab and went to my "four-star" hotel. It had been recommended as 'the only place someone coming from the civilized world should stay.'

"Are you sure this is the place?" I asked the cab driver when he stopped in front of at what seemed to be the ruins of a building post World War II."

"Yep, this is the place."

"But it is supposed to be a four-star hotel."

"Well, the name of the hotel is Four Stars, if that helps." He said.

I collected my belonging, entered the hotel, paid a week in advance, and was given the key to my room.

"Third floor." The ugly dude at the reception desk waved me off. The key was three inches long and heavy. It could easily cause astonishment to a fifth-grade class on a field trip to a museum. I was drenched in sweat and about to have a heat stroke, but nobody ever offered to help me. Not the airport staff, taxi driver or hotel personnel. There was no doorman.

"Where's the elevator?" I asked, knowing the answer.

"No such a thing here. The stairs are to your left."

I dragged the bags upstairs, instead of leaving one behind and coming back to retrieve it later, because I was certain that it wouldn't be there if I did so. After three attempts to unlock the door, I was able to manage the intricacies of the lock and opened the door to a plain smelly bedroom. It had a single bed with a two-inch mattress, filled with who-knows-what, a small sink and a bathroom that maybe had been white a long time ago. I turned the rusty shower valve on and this putrid brown liquid came from it. There was no telephone in the room, so…I gagged my way to the front desk and asked the ugly guy to check it out for me. He told me that he was on his own and could not leave the front desk alone. He would send a handyman to check the problem once he could get a hold of him.

One hour later, someone knocked on the door. The handyman managed to be uglier than his front desk counterpart and was carrying a mallet in his right hand.

"What tha plobrem?"

"Uh? The shower. The water is brown and stinky."

The guy looked at me as if I were a lunatic; shook his head, opened the shower and the fetid liquid poured out of it.

I pointed to the water with my left hand. "You see?"

"So… what tha plobrem?"

I wanted to cry. The concept of clear or potable water hadn't made it to this town.

The first night was awaking nightmare. The mattress felt and sounded like it was filled with dry corn husks. I could even hear critters crawling inside of it. Not to mention that mosquitos and flies were flying over my head as if they were waiting for command orders to attack. Despite my vigilance, the morning came with several bites and rashes.

"It looks like you haven't brought a mosquito net with you." A pilot at the airport asked me when he saw the evidence on my arms. "The insects will feast on you."

The mosquito net was positively my best investment in the Amazon, together with a new pricey 4-inch mattress I got delivered to the hotel, part of an advance payment my new bosses gave me. I was about to throw the creepy crawler nest in the garbage can behind the hotel, and set it on fire when a local guy came and asked me why I was going to get rid of a perfectly shaped mattress. Without another word, I gave it to him and his two-tooth smile showed me much appreciation.

Pilots are used to saying that flying is defined as hours of boredom with moments of sheer terror; but I never felt that way until I started flying in the Amazon. Flying there was beyond scary. Right before my introductory flight, in a single engine airplane, while I was doing my pre-flight duties, a pile of stuff was dropped beside the airplane (everything you can imagine, from pots to pigs). I asked the people on the ramp how many trips would be necessary to take the pile. They flashed those toothless smiles at me and shook their heads, as if I had just made a funny comment.

A few moments later, the pilot in charge of the flight, my flight evaluator, arrived bringing three passengers.

"Let's load this thing."

"What?" I asked.

"What? Do you expect the ramp crew to load the aircraft?" Before I could reply, he added. "They wouldn't know how to balance the CG."

"No... I didn't know we would have passengers too. How

much freight are we leaving behind?"

"What are you talking about... we're not leaving anything be-hind."

He put two passengers against the right wall, fenced them with a wall of little crates with chickens, put another passenger on the rear seat and engulfed him with boxes of food, placed a couple of propane tanks in the middle, squeezed bags of beans between them, and filled the gaps with loose clothes. He, then, managed to put a bicycle between the ceiling and the tanks. Some bags of cement were put on top of the only empty seat and that served as support for two massive chainsaws. The pig would have to travel in a vertical position since his crate lost its priority. Every space left was filled with softer stuff.

"Aren't we too heavy?" I dared to ask.

The pilot stepped back, looked at the landing gear with one eye closed, looked at the tail and said, "We're still good."

"But you're not even counting our weight?"

"Relax... we will be fine."

I didn't relax. And I found out I would not relax for the next several months. It was 90°F already and getting warmer. In any civilized part of the world, this would constitute in a suicide mission. In the Amazon, that was just the way things worked.

I had to bring the power lever almost to the full forward position to get the airplane rolling for taxing.

Thankfully, White River of Acre had a 7,000-foot runway, which was considered to be very long, for the region's standards, and the treetops had been cut at the end of the runway. We used every inch of the runway to get airborne and then we established a daunting 300-foot per minute rate of climb. Any attempt to get a better rate of climb and the stall warning started telling us that the treetops were calling our names. It was when the airplane would not climb anymore that we would consider our cruise altitude, at whatever number of feet above the trees that was. We then,

111

would look for references (rivers, clearings in the jungle or stars at night) to give us any clue about our position. GPS technology had not arrived at the Amazon region yet. The destinations were no more hospitable than the surface of Mars. The "runways" were openings near settlements in the middle of the jungle, barely clearing the wingtips of the airplane.

I knew that there would be no way we could carry similar loads back, but we never had too. People would only go to the urban areas to buy supplies. And these were deprived folks. Even the word "underprivileged" doesn't do justice to the conditions they lived in. There were no roads to and from the settlements. The only way out would be by boat or plane. A boat trip could take weeks, a round-trip could take a full month. Why someone who was not a true native would decide to live in such a hostile environment, was an enigma to me.

While in flight, during level cruise, I took advantage of the one-on-one attention and asked my pilot-guide all the questions I should have researched before embarking on such adventure.

"What do you do for fun on your time off?"

He shrugged his shoulders and made a face as if I had asked him what he was breathing, "B and H."

"Uh?"

"Booze and hookers."

What was I expecting? A book club?

"I know all the good hookers in town. Don't go straight to the better-looking ones, you will regret it later. There are some clean ones, they are not very attractive but all you have to do is close your eyes. I will recommend some for you."

"It's okay... I am not much of a B and H person, anyway."

"Ha... you say that now; but the jungle has a way of changing people."

I didn't like his demeanor at all and decided to change the subject.

112

"Do a lot of accidents happen here?"

"Define 'accidents.' Remember, this is the Wild West of Aviation; a totally different world from the one you came from. We lose pilots every month or two." He sneered, "That's how you got a chance to come here, anyway." Then, added in a more serious tone, "Maintenance is almost non-existent; they expect you to fix things yourself and keep the airplane airworthy. You will see, problems arise from nowhere and the competition plays dirty."

"What if we have to make a crash landing on the edge of a river?"

"You're gone!" He said without much thought, "Did you see any Emergency Locator Transmitter during your pre-flight?"

"I was going to ask you that. I couldn't find one."

"Of course, you couldn't... because none of our airplanes have one." He sneered, "Keep this in mind, if you survive a crash landing here, nobody is coming after you, and even if they came, at that point you will probably already have become some creature's dinner."

"Really?"

"Welcome to the jungle, kiddo."

I became terribly quiet, all of a sudden. He saw my reaction to his words and decided to cheer me up.

"Nah... I wouldn't sweat the big creatures. It's either the sabotage from the competition or the tiny little critters that will kill you."

I had many more questions, but after that last comment, I was afraid of hearing more disturbing answers.

Again, I wanted to quit. Except that, knowing that this time was going to be harder, I left no exit for myself. After the one-way airplane ticket and the advance pay for accommodations, I had no money left; which meant, I would have to bite the bullet.

After a couple of months doing the job, I started to feel a little bit less uncomfortable with the situation, but the goal was to leave the area by the end of the year. The pay was outstanding and it was easy to save because there was nothing worth spending it on, unless you wanted to get drunk or risk getting STDs. The money in itself was the only reason to stay, but still, better alive and unemployed than dead on the job.

In the time I spent in the Amazon, I witnessed so many situations which are hard to describe and even harder to believe. I saw kids living with parasitic diseases that no human being should ever experience, like the bacteria that eats the gummy flesh of one's body or the kissing bug disease that leads to enlargement of the ventricles of one's heart. When I got in the Amazon, I used to quietly cry of remorse in my hotel room because of the decision I had made. In a few weeks, my crying became less selfish. I would cry for the kids I'd see on a daily basis, who had no palate or whose engorged hearts were causing a slow and painful death.

Maybe humans shouldn't be here." It was a thought that was constantly in my mind.

And then, there were the shenanigans created by the flying humans. The **Corisco** tale would be hard to believe if I hadn't watched it with my own eyes. The brakes of a Piper Cherokee, from one of our competitors, had gone bad in one of the settlements. Every bush pilot knew that the only way to takeoff from the short runway was to bring the throttle to full power while holding the brakes in order to accumulate energy, and then release the brakes.

Since I knew that the pilot would not be able to do that, I offered him a ride back to White River, where he could get new brakes and fly back with one of this company pilots to the settlement the next day. But given that the bosses of our companies were arch enemies, he rejected the idea.

I flew to my next settlement, thirty minutes away, where all the air taxi companies had aviation gas available in separate barrels to refuel our planes so that we would have enough to get back to White River. While refueling my own airplane, I was telling one of our ramp guys about the Cherokee predicament in the other settlement, when all of a sudden, we saw it approaching and flying a couple of circles over the airstrip. The jungle absorbs sounds and, most of time, you can't hear an airplane approaching until it is above you.

"I can't believe this!"

"You said he has no brakes?"

"Yeah, no brake action, the pads were gone. I wonder how he took off from the other settlement."

The ramp guy asked, "Why didn't he fly straight to White River?"

"Like me, he doesn't have enough fuel. I bet he's here to get some."

"But if he has no brakes, how is he going to land here?"

As we were wondering, we saw a group of people by the runway. My intrigued ramp guy went to see what the commotion was all about and soon returned with news.

"You guys won't believe this!"

"What?"

"The word is that the aircraft still has no brakes, and the owner of the company asked his loader here to find a couple of strong folks to help stop the airplane after it touches down."

"Stop the airplane? How?"

"By trying to grab and hold the wing. He offered ten bucks for every person who is willing to help."

"You're right. I don't believe it."

I thought the loader would find no takers, but that kind of money goes a long way for those who have nothing. All of a sudden, a mini crowd gathered beside the runway. The helpers spaced themselves, at every 50 feet along the sides of the airstrip. I wanted to stop the madness but my ramp guy advised me not to mess with those people. They'd do anything for ten bucks.

So, right in front of us, the Cherokee approached to land. It touched down on the first feet of the airstrip and was pretty fast for the first helpers to put their hands on it. One helper in the middle right side of the strip tried to jump on the wing as it passed by. Alas, his judgment of the airplane speed was off and the wing got him right at chest level, he flew backwards and hit the back of his head so hard against the ground that we could hear the cracking of his skull. He died on the spot.

Another helper had his forehead sliced by the left strobe light mirror, and a third had his arm broken by the horizontal stabilizer. Finally, the "shrewder helpers," who had positioned themselves at the last third of the airstrip, were able to stop the airplane before it hit the stumps and trees at the end. Final tally: one dead, two serious hurt and six guys with big bruises.

Despite the fact that I was making good money and had planned to stay another four months, the last straw happened two weeks after the event with the Cherokee. As I mentioned, even though pilots flew for different companies, we shared a camaraderie that was stronger than our employers' rivalry. I took off one morning, followed by a similar aircraft flown by Tony, one of our competitors, thirty minutes behind, and then another one of our pilots who was about one hour behind Tony, heading to the same settlement.

I landed and had two hours before heading to the next settlement. Thirty minutes passed and no signs of the rival airplane. One hour and twenty-five minutes passed and then our second pilot landed.

"Didn't Tony takeoff?" I asked my coworker, as soon as his door opened.

"He did," the pilot stated, "Half an hour after you, as always. Why? Isn't he here?"

"No, he isn't."

"Maybe he went direct to the second settlement."

"Yeah, maybe."

I helped unload the plane and went to the tiny, closet-sized office of the competition. Their dispatcher/loader was on the phone, sweating under a fan as big as the office itself.

He lifted his head and somehow seemed happy to see us. He was never well-mannered, often referring to us as "the dumb foes." Covering the transmitter end of the rotary phone handset, he asked, "Have you guys seen or heard from Tony?"

"No, that's why we're here."

His face went blank and the fake refinement vanished from his body. He took his hand off the transmitter and continued talking to whoever he was talking to before, as if we weren't there.

"The foes haven't seen him either... I wouldn't be surprised if they sabotaged his aircraft. Let me know if he gets there."

Hanging up the phone, he shook his head and waved us out of the boxy office.

"Did Tony's airplane have an Emergency Locator Transmitter?" I asked as we were leaving the office.

"ELT? Who has money for that kind of thing? You are really a dumb foe." He replied.

"Do you think they will call Search & Rescue?" I turned to my coworker.

"Are you still in La-La-Land?" the other pilot scolded me.

"We could fly back and do a quick search of the area."

"Yeah, it's official! You're still in La-La-Land. Do you think the boss would let us do that?"

"But somebody has to do something." I pleaded.

"Sorry, man. I've seen this so many times. It's over for him. Say a little prayer."

Tony, his airplane and his passengers were never found.

Feeling that I could become the next Tony, three days later I converted all my earnings into an airline ticket and left the Amazon for good, without a spare dime in my pocket. My only inheritances were a mosquito net and some scars on my soul.

CHAPTER FIFTEEN
The Proposal

The year following my Amazon adventure saw the country's economy tank even more, with high inflation and unemployment. I couldn't find any commercial pilot jobs in the industrialized areas and had to go back to flight instructing. Even though there were enough students to keep me flying three times a week (and I was accruing hours toward my air transport pilot certificate), the money was not enough for me to rent a place, and I went back to living with my parents.

One day, as my family and I had just sat at the dining room table to have lunch, the phone rang (as it was always the case when my dad had a chance to swing by the house, to get a hot meal).

"Let's not answer it." Dad said, "It's probably one of my clients wondering what time I am going to deliver his order." My father loathed being interrupted during mealtimes.

We let the phone ring its twelve traditional rings until it stopped. A minute later, it started again, "RIIIIIIIIIING!"

"It must be something important." Mom remarked.

"If you're really curious, go ahead." Dad said.

As she left the table to answer the phone, dad cleaned his mouth with his napkin, a bit exasperated, "I am pretty sure it's a client. They know it's lunch time… why?'

We could hear mom picking up the phone in the living room.

"Hello?" pause, "Yes, it is," pause, "Senior or junior?" pause, "Oh... just a second."

She came back to the dining room as my dad started to get up, "It's actually for Junior."

"For me?" I thought it was the flight school rescheduling a student.

"Hello?"

The voice on the other side of the line was not familiar, "Joey Uliana... Junior?"

"This is he."

"Listen, you don't know me, but your name came up and we decided to give you a chance. You are a commercial pilot with IFR and multi-engine certificates, correct?"

"That's right. Who is this?"

"Listen... we have a proposal for you?"

Who are 'we'? I thought.

"Proposal? A job?"

"Yes... it's a job. We have a nice airplane we would like you to fly?"

"What kind of airplane? Where?"

"It's a Beech Baron 58 TC... you'd be flying it from the border of Brazil and Bolivia to Colombia and then back."

"Say what?"

"Listen carefully. You fly this beautiful airplane to our destination. Once there, we will load the cargo..."

"What kind of cargo?" I interrupted the man.

"There's no need for you to know what kind of cargo it is. Just that it is not ammunition or explosives, and the airplane will not be overloaded."

"But, but..."

"Then, you fly back to the origin airport, we offload the cargo and guess what?"

119

"What?"

"After we offload the cargo, you keep it."

"Keep it? Keep what? The cargo?"

"The airplane. The airplane will be yours, as payment for the job."

Long pause now.

Then I started laughing, nervous laughter, and said, "Wait a minute! Who is this? It's a prank, right? Who asked you to call me? It was Ed, wasn't it? Good one, but tell him that I am not falling for it."

"Who is Ed?" The voice on the other side of the line asked in a dry tone.

I felt the hair in the back of my neck sticking up and a lone drop of sweat fell out of my temple, "Are you seriously offering me an airplane for a job?"

I looked toward the dining room and both my parents had their heads sticking out and tilted by the dining room door, trying to make sense of what I was saying to the person on the other side of the line.

"Yes sir. That's the offer. You do your part, we do our part and the airplane is yours, no strings attached."

If you want to mess with the head of a youngster that has no more than 200 dollars in his bank account, has to take public transportation to work, and lives with his parents, offer him a car. If you want to drive him/her insane, offer an airplane.

I pointed to the phone frantically, covered it with my left hand and whispered to my parents, "This guy is offering me an airplane in exchange of some flying." My parents' faces showed more concern than wonder.

I knew what to do, of course. I just wanted to taste the moment for more than a moment.

I cleaned my throat and spoke as a grown up.

"Wow... I'd like to thank you for thinking of me for such a job, but I will have to decline at this time." "

"You sure? It's a brand-new Baron... and it can be all yours after a few hours of flying."

He was twisting my arm, and mind, "Yeah, I'm positive."

"Not a problem. We're going to call the next pilot on the list."

I felt that he was about to hang up and said quickly, "By the way... who do I owe the honor of this call? Who referred me?"

I knew that there would be no way he would tell me. There was a long pause on his side now, as if he had just put the phone down and was debating with himself whether to tell me or not, laughing at my boldness for asking.

I was expecting to hear a click and the phone going mute, but heard a "Humph," and then, before hanging up, he said with a lot of pride in his voice, "It would be with the compliments of Mr. Pablo Escobar."

"Ah... okay. Thanks for let..." He hung up before I could complete the sentence.

I just stood there. It took a couple of minutes for me to put the phone back in its cradle.

History showed that I made the right decision; but boy oh boy, talk about temptation.

CHAPTER SIXTEEN
Missing Man

In order to die… you're just required to be living.

I remember staring at two posters from the Service of Investigation and Prevention of Aeronautical Accidents (SIPAER), on the wall of a flight school; the first one was a pilot bragging to an angel in heaven, "I have been flying for more than 30 years, and I have had only one accident."

The other poster was a series of cartoons alluding to how people conceal their mistakes. First cartoon was of a cook that had accidentally burnt his main dish. He hid the charcoaled crust by pouring sauce on top of it, the caption read, "Cooks' mistakes are covered with sauce." The second one was an architectural design blemish on a building; the architect hid it by planting a tree in front of it; the caption read, "Architects mistakes are covered with plants. The last one was a cemetery worker covering a grave; the caption read, "Pilots' mistakes are covered with dirt."

In the community I was raised, death was something far away, something that only happened to someone's grandparents or great-grandparents.

That notion changed when I entered the aviation world.

It was a lazy Monday morning, as Monday mornings tend to be, and everyone in our commercial pilot course entered the classroom dragging their feet. Mr. Ruddick, the Advanced Aero-dynamics ground instructor, entered the room wearing a much more subdued face than what we were used to seeing. After any given weekend, it normally took a couple of minutes to get every-one focused; there were ten chats going on at once, paper planes crossing from one side of the classroom to the other; we were filled with total and innocent foolishness. Mr. Ruddick often joined the natter for a few minutes, easing his control over the class. This time though, he was not carrying his usual happy-go-lucky demeanor.

"Guys, guys, GUYS... LISTEN!"

Ruddick never used to raise his voice, so the room became instantly and eerily quiet. He cleared his throat, "Hem...you're new to this, so I will break the news to you as it is, no point in sugar-coating."

We looked at each other without moving our heads.

"You must know that... in our line of business, there will be sudden and sometimes unexplainable departures." He scanned the room before continuing, probably shocked by how fast it had become dead silent, "And by 'departures,' I mean deaths."

He started pacing in front of the long blackboard we had on a slightly raised platform. "We share the good and bad times to-gether, and become brothers-in-arms, friends for life..."

I looked around, quickly doing a head count. There were two guys missing. I clinched my jaw.

"...and the only way to avoid losing a friend, is making a de-liberate choice of not having one or not being one."

More morbid silence.

His eyes watered and his chin trembled before he spoke the words that no one wanted to hear, he spilled it out in one breath.

"There has been an accident this morning. Unfortunately, Leonard passed away."

Nobody knew him as Leonard. For us, he was "Spaghetti" or

simply "Ghetti," a nickname derived by his long body shape and his appetite for pasta. He used to fly his dad's Piper Cherokee 140 from a small dirt runway located in a rural town to the big city, every Monday, and then back to the town every Friday.

The news that Ghetti had **bought the farm** devastated the class. It wasn't an eighty-year-old man dying of normal causes, or a forty-year-old dying from a serious illness. It was our classmate and friend, the tall, skinny eighteen-year-old boy with freckles dominating his light complexion, an effortless smile and neatly combed hair overloaded with gel, which we used to joke that was licked by a cow every morning. And what killed him was not a disease or an automobile accident; it was our cause, our passion, our future profession: aviation.

"Today's class is canceled... in memory of Leonard," the instructor said. He might as well have said it in an outlandish idiom because we had stop listening. We just sat there, some in deep thoughts, others silently crying, nobody moving.

That's when I learned that just because you're totally devoted to a cause, it doesn't mean that it can't harm you (lethally).

It happened again and again. Friends and acquaintances started dropping from the skies like flies. Aviation, still a new innovation for humans, was unforgiving.

Am I next? It was an insistent thought, demanding me to quit or else.

Then, it hit too close to home. I had just started a job as a corporate pilot for a small company. After being gone for two straight weeks, the company's driver dropped me off at home and I was surprised to see my parents waiting for me at the gate.

They must really be missing me.

"Hi mom, hi dad!"

They nodded their heads and hugged me tighter than usual. I concluded that they had something to tell me, but I didn't push the matter.

"Is everything alright? Where's Ginger (my sister)?" I asked as casually as I could, to whoever wanted to answer.

"She's at the dancing studio," said mom.

Good! Her reply brought a little of peace of mind, as my dad carried my bags and put them in my room. He was quieter than usual, by this time he would have already asked a bunch of questions about my trip. The man who once couldn't conceive the idea that his own son wanted to become a pilot, now was excited with my world, so different from his own.

Not that day though, and I wondered why.

I took a long shower while my magnificent mom arranged something for me to eat. One gets tired of eating on the road all the time, and I was looking forward to a homemade meal, cooked with care.

My parents sat at the table with me as I ate frantically. They kept staring at me the whole time.

"I think I am going to take a nap," I said after the meal. "I'm a bit tired."

Mom followed me close to the room with a somber look, while dad stayed in the kitchen.

"OK... what is it?" I spun around and asked, "Did someone die?" My tone was a bit acerbic, maybe because I was tired, maybe because I was scared. Either way, the mordant question did not expect to have an affirmative answer.

Her nodding almost knocked me cold. I sat on the edge of my bed by reflex.

"Oh please, mom... don't tell me it's... (I named three of my best friends)."

She looked away and I saw the tears rolling from her face.

My room was painted like the sky, with some puffy clouds to remind me of home. In that moment, a million thoughts occurred at the same time; before she could mention the name, I relived my friendship with three of the most wonderful human beings I had ever met, trying to foolishly convince myself that it was not him or him or him.

Then, the short vowel came out of her mouth.

"Ed."

It was unacceptable. It was not possible that happiness was going to be stolen from our world. I couldn't even start to try to describe this human being. Ed was a smile that someone had made into a person.

"When?" the saltiness of my own tears reached my mouth.

"It's been almost a week," mom said, "we knew there was no TV in the ranch you were staying, and we didn't want you to get upset to the point that you wouldn't be able to fly the plane back safely."

Now, I was upset... not sure with what or who. I knew that his departure would leave a big void in many lives, as it happens with those that are loved by each person they touch.

A few days later, I attended a service in his honor. To witness his parents suffering has been one of the most painful emotions I have felt in life, and that prompted me to vow to never make my own parents go through that kind of pain, no matter what.

The explanations and conclusions for Ed's accident are still vague to this day. Many theories were formed to explain why his aircraft broke apart in midair. As a result, some of our closest pilot friends stopped flying altogether. I did not become afraid of flying, as I have never been afraid of dying. His departure took something from me though, but it gave me something else in return.

As it is in life, in aviation, it's vital to learn from other people's mistakes because most of time you don't get a second chance. That's why pilots read aviation accident reports; it's not because we nurture a morbid side, but because by analyzing what was done wrong once, we can avoid repeating it (and be covered with dirt).

I have lost almost a dozen friends to aviation accidents. Each

of them paved my way to be a safer pilot; each of them a remind-
er that mountains are harder than clouds, that mother nature always has the last say, and that it is important to be safe and legal,
in that order (better off explaining a mishap to an aviation inspector than to an angel).

Yet, I have reached a point where I believe that nobody truly
dies. Our existence continues and we follow our magnificent journey after our mission here is over.

To live in the hearts we leave behind, is not to die

CHAPTER SEVENTEEN
Mister Zig

Some of the stories in this book have a common theme, "If I hadn't lived it, I wouldn't believe it." That's the case with Mister Zig. He could easily be the fruit of my imagination, such an allegorical character he turned out to be. I came to know him and his unstoppable zest for life through the world of flying.

A friend had introduced me to an aviation sales representative called Mr. Leon, during a safety symposium, in the early 1990s. I noticed that the sales representative was well connected and I told him I was looking for jobs, just in case he sold an aircraft and needed a pilot to go with it. It worked; a few weeks later, he called asking me if I would be interested in flying for a local farmer. In that time, soy farmers, in the southern states of Brazil, made a lot of money, and started buying land in other regions of the country. The preferred means of transportation was small private airplanes, that not only could land on short dirt strips but also be available anytime. Mr. Leon scheduled a local flight, so that I could demonstrate my proficiency to the farmer.

I got to the local airport 40 minutes earlier than our ETD and started doing the pre-flight inspection in the assigned twin-engine Piper Seneca. Mr. Leon arrived right on time, in a new white Chevy, wearing a flawless suit. Ten minutes later, this 6-foot tall, long-bearded man, who looked as if he had just gone through a dust storm, arrived out of the blue and started talking to Mr. Leon. I thought it strange to see a homeless person at the airport, a location so detached from the city. Still, it was obvious that he approached the man in the suit to solicit money.

From afar, I saw Mr. Leon gesture to me to get in the airplane and get ready.

I slid to the left seat, and ran the 'Before Start,' checklist when Mr. Leon and "Pig-Pen" walked toward the airplane.

As Mr. Leon got up the right wing to get to the right seat, the grimy fella walked around the airplane, opened the back door and sat in the left back seat, put his seatbelt on and closed the door.

Are we going to take the homeless guy flying? He's going to soil the entire interior. He even smells!

I looked at Mr. Leon with a shocking expression, waiting for an explanation, but he just said, "Let's go. Start this thing."

I started, taxied, took off and we flew eastward for twenty minutes; then, abiding by his request, we came back and I performed two Touch-and-Gos and a full stop landing. During the entire flight, I couldn't help thinking about the dirty chap and Mr. Leon's actions.

Who invites a bum to go on a proficiency check flight? Would it be possible that this guy works for the owner?

The flight ended, I shut the engines down and began checking the post-flight items in the checklist, while Mr. Leon and the dirt man exited the airplane and started talking outside. When I got off the airplane, the dirt man walked toward me, opened a big smile (a smile that I would soon learn to admire), gave me a hand-breaking handshake and simply said, "Good job."

Then he waved to Mr. Leon, walked to the parking lot, got into a red Ferrari and drove away, like a maniac.

Mr. Leon approached me, put his hand on my left shoulder, giggling at my dropped jaw and said, "That's Mr. Zig, if you haven't figured it out yet."

"Uh?"

"He is the owner of the aircraft. You're hired."

It took no time for me to learn that Mr. Zig was a self-made German farmer who lived in a detached Teutonic community 40 miles from the city airport. Like many farmers in the southern region of Brazil, Mr. Zig had prospered to a financial point that allowed him to explore virgin and fertile soil in other parts of the country. He was able to afford massive spreads of land that were located respectively 800 and 1500 miles away from his main farm. Like many other farmers, the only efficient way to reach his farms was by private airplane; unlike most farmers, he had a passion for aviation.

I also soon learned that he was a bit insane when it came to efficiency; his main pet-peeve was 'waste of time.' After our first trip together, it became quite clear that he had tendencies toward pushing the envelope, both the pilot's and the aircraft's. For every time I would raise concerns about the weather, he always would counter with, "I know you can do it, captain."

When Mr. Zig bought the Piper Seneca, he was given the option to install a weather radar or a GPS. He told Mr. Leon that his budget for the aircraft would allow for only one of those add-ons. He opted for the latter, which was not the smartest choice considering that most flights were conducted in an area known as the thunderstorm belt.

In the three years I flew for Mr. Zig, there were some memorable flights, but not all of them resulted in inspirational memories.

I ended up doing a lot of things against my better judgment in that Seneca, and later paid a price for them with two bouts of gastritis. Among the uncomfortable shenanigans were: landings in crosswinds that almost exceeded my ability and the aircraft's performance; two engine-out emergency landings and an encounter with an embedded thunderstorm which almost caused me to buy the farm.

There was this time we landed at his northernmost farm, which was at least 200 miles from any town, and the monsoon season decided to arrive early and dumped a ton of rain, turning the dirty runway into a rectangular brown lake. Mr. Zig started to become apprehensive on our third day there.

"We have to find a solution to get out of here. I still have to go back to farm #2 before we return home."

"Well, unless we turn the Seneca into an amphibian airplane, we are stuck here for a while."

He looked through me, and I saw the light bulb shining on top of his head while a wide smile formed.

"Why are you smiling?"

"I am going to 'make' another runway."

Before I could say anything, he jumped on a big Massey Ferguson tractor, ordered some of his employees to do the same and they started to pave a new runway. In a couple of hours, they made a strip long enough for our departure and towed the airplane there; but, to my complete relief, the weather got even worse and the visibility dropped to almost zero.

"We're leaving first thing in the morning," he said.

"Provided that the weather gets better." I noted.

"It will be."

The next morning, as soon as there was enough light to see outside, he woke me up and said, "Let's go, there's a hole in the sky."

"Uh?!" I lifted my head up, still confused for being awaken in such a sudden matter, just to see him storming out of the door with his bag and MY bag.

I ran after him shouting, "I need to brush my teeth and I need to change."

He didn't even turn around, "No time for it. That hole may

close soon."

And yet, there was a tiny hole in the clouds, and it would not last.

So, I got in the airplane still in my pajamas, fired the engines, took off from the new soft runway, pointed my nose toward the hole, got on top of the clouds and turned toward Brasilia, the capital of Brazil, where we generally stopped for fuel.

Two hours later, my wheels touched the tarmac of SBBS (Brasilia Intl. Airport) and I taxied up to the main FBO's gas service station. As fate would have it, there was a Department of Civil Aviation inspector there (their equivalent of an FAA), doing random ramp checks. He aimed straight at my airplane as soon as I shut the engines down. Mr. Zig, foreseeing the conflict, slid off the wing and told me he was going to get some coffee, even though I knew he was not a coffee drinker. The inspector didn't miss a beat. He eyed me in the cockpit and asked pointblank, "Do you hold a pilot's license?"

"Yes, sir."

"What are you doing, flying in your pajamas? What kind of professional are you?"

I stammered some words, trying to explain a situation that for me was both sad and comical at the same time, but he would have none of it, pointed to the building beside the FBO and ordered, "Meet me in my office in 10 minutes, in a decent pilot uniform, if you have one."

That day, I got lectured on what a disgrace I was to the aviation community.

Another story, which became one for the records, has to do with one of the toughest flights of my life. If only I knew then what I know now.

The phone rang once, twice, five, ten times before I picked it up.

"Hello."

"Hello... Captain?"

"Yep," I answered, knowing already who was on the other side of the line.

"I know it's your day off, but..."

"Yes?"

"We have a mercy flight." The voice waited for my reply, and when it didn't come, it continued, "Are you up for it?"

Oh man... it's my day-off. We arrived yesterday from a long flight. And the autopilot is inoperative. Why, why, why?

"Boss...," my better side started, "...how many times do I have to tell you that I am always available for mercy flights?"

A 'mercy flight' is the air transport of a seriously ill or injured person from an isolated community to the hospital, preferably in an urban area. It demands voluntary contributions from all parties involved. An airplane owner donates the aircraft and fuel for the flight while the pilot donates their time and skill. In other words, in countries where there are no aerial emergency evacuation service or air ambulances, no one gets paid. It's similar to "Doctors without Borders," but instead of taking a doctor to patients in remote areas, pilots bring patients from remote areas to the hospitals. In many parts of the world, mercy flights make the difference between life and death.

"Ok, ok... I thought it would be polite to ask first," Mr. Zig said. "Here's what we know so far... a truck driver from our area crashed his big rig while carrying supplies on his way to Xingu, 14 miles east of the indigenous reservation of Xavantina. They took him to some kind of infirmary, in a village, but his injuries are life-threatening, and he needs to be taken to a hospital immediately, preferably back here."

"Back here?" I looked at my watch, "We're talking almost 1,800 miles round trip, and it's already noon and..."

"I know, I know. There are no airports with runway lights in a

133

300-mile radius. You have to act quickly. Refuel somewhere before you get there, land before sunset, get him in the airplane and
take off while there's still light in the sky."

"I'm out the door now." I hung up without goodbyes, put my
uniform on, picked my flight bag, hugged mom and was about to
grab my keys when the phone rang once again.

It was Mr. Zig again, "Another thing... take a copilot with you.
You know, with the autopilot not working... there are lots of
'hangar rats' at the airport. Pick one of them; a copilot may come
handy for the long flight."

"Got it! By the way, can you please call our mechanic and tell
him to take the back seats out the airplane."

"I've already cal..." I didn't even let him finish the sentence. I
hopped on my brownish Honda 125cc motorcycle and rode the 12
miles that separated my parents' house from the airport.

On the way to the airport, I thought about a dozen guys I
could pick to be my copilot. Most of them were just like me when I
was struggling to make ends meet. Johnny was the youngest one
in the pack of wannabe pilots and the one that seemed to need
flying hours the most. What the scrawny lad lacked in maturity; he
compensated for in enthusiasm, not to mention that his house
was on the way.

I stopped in front of a wooden structure that looked like one of
the three little pigs' houses after the wolf had blown it away, and
honked a couple of times.

No answer

"Johnny."

A rachitic woman, with more wrinkles in her lips than teeth in
her mouth, emerged from one of the windows, "Johnny ain't here."

"Wher..."

She pointed toward the airport.

"He's going on a trip," I shouted as I started the motorcycle.

At the hangar, Johnny was already helping Mike, the mechanic, to unscrew and take out the last back seat in the Seneca.

"How did you know?" I asked.

"How did I know what?"

"That you were going with me on this trip?"

"Are you kidding me?" His face lit up. "That's awesome! I have to go home and pack my bag and..."

"There's no time for that."

"But I am wearing shorts and sneakers."

"I have an extra pair." I tossed him a pilot's shirt and navy pants. "They will be big on you, but you'll look official." I had learned my lesson after the pajama episode.

Johnny's eyes lit up, he was in and out of the men's room within a minute, walking on the tarmac as if it were a catwalk. My uniform was two sizes too big for his frame, but he didn't care.

"Wow... Johnny, you look different in human clothes." The mechanic teased him.

He jumped in the right seat, stuck his thumbs up and opened a wide grin.

I shook my head. "You have to let me get in first, airhead!"

During the first leg of the flight, we calculated that we should land in a city called Heron's Bar to refuel; then, continue to Xavantina, pick up the wounded driver, fly straight back to our home airport, and hope that we would not have to go to any alternate airport as we probably would not be able to make one.

The flight up to Heron's Bar was uneventful and everything worked as planned. Stop, refuel to the rim and go. We arrived in Xavantina 30 minutes before sunset, and it looked like all 253 of its indigenous inhabitants and two missionaries were at the short and narrow dirt airstrip, waiting for us.

"Eguahé porá!" A tall, well-nurtured gracious native greeted us, with his right fist against his chest.

"Uh?"

"He is welcoming you. He is Cacique Huanti, the head of this tribe." A missionary interjected, "And I am Larry Matthews."

"Hello Mr. Matthews." I said, and then turned to the indigenous leader and put my right fist on my chest and bowed.

"Don't bow," said the missionary, "and call me Larry."

I turned to him, "Forgive our rush, but there's no time to waste. Where's the driver?"

Larry's right eyebrow arched as he extended the palm of his right hand to an old 4x4 Toyota. There was what looked to be like a coffin, sticking of the back door.

I opened my arms and looked to Johnny, who was watching everything unfold from inside the airplane.

"He's there," Larry assured. "We sealed the coffin because it's starting to decompose. But don't worry... we covered the body with a plant similar to lavender, to cover the stench. Do you want us to open it?"

"No," I said, in a bit of shock. "What are you talking about? Decompose? When did he die?"

"We don't know. He was already dead when we got to the crash scene. Gladly we found them before a jaguar did... lots of those here. They could've easily become its meal," Larry said. "Didn't you know he was dead?"

"No. We were sent here to pick him up and take him to a hospital back home."

"Oh... they were probably thinking about his wife."

"I beg your pardon?"

"We found his wife alive. She is still in the village. She doesn't know her husband's dead."

"Nobody said anything about a wife. I wasn't told about someone else traveling with him."

Larry didn't care if I had been properly briefed about the situation or not, and said, "She is in serious pain."

My head started spinning.

"Okay, here's what we are going to do... Can some of the in-digenous fellas here help Johnny load and secure the coffin in the airplane, while we go to check on the wife?"

"Certainly, we can do that. But she has to go with you, or else she will die here. We don't have the meds to treat such injuries."

They unloaded the coffin from the back of the Toyota truck and Larry took me to the village where the women were watching over the wife. When we got there, she was convulsing and out of her senses, screaming in pain.

"Do you have a stretcher I can take with me? I asked.

"A stretcher?" Larry looked at me as if I had asked him if he had a giant golden saucer.

"Yeah... like a gurney."

"Of course not. We have nothing of the sort here."

I wiped the sweat from my forehead and neck, "Where is the nearest phone located?"

"Phone?"

"Yes... telephone." I was getting a bit exasperated.

"Six hours by car from here, in New Vienna. But most of the time, it doesn't work."

The sun was starting to touch the torrid horizon. "There's no time for anything, anyway. Let's load her beside the..."

Larry leaned down and interrupted me with a whispered, "I think it would be wise to cover the coffin with some cloth and then load her on top of it, so she will not be able to see it."

We put the woman on the back of the Toyota pickup, and drove back to the airstrip. Every bump on the road made the woman shriek so sharply that her pain echoed in my soul.

Noticing my discomfort, Larry said, "I am going to give her co-ca leaf tea before you guys take off... that will make her pass out."

"Coca leaf tea? Is it going to work, really?"

"I think it will."

After securing the makeshift-coffin to the floor of the aircraft, we covered it with a thin blanket and tied the truck driver's wife on top of it. We were in a big rush. In the twilight, everything was done without much attention to detail. Johnny was starting to gag from the foul smell of the dead and injured bodies.

I asked Larry to get the indigenous people to light up some torches and put at the far end and the sides of the runway, so that I could have an idea where it ended. Any sign of sunlight had been swallowed by darkness.

The takeoff was tense, and I let go a sigh of relief once the wheels left the ground.

During the climb out, passing five thousand feet, I relaxed a little bit more and said, "What a mess, uh? Can you grab the flashlight under your seat and check our passenger?"

After no reply from the right seat, I spoke again. "Johnny, are you with me?"

"Uh, ye-ah." He replied with a weak voice.

"You haven't said a word since we landed in Xavantina."

Johnny's face was probably paler than the deceased driver in the coffin. He grabbed the flashlight, pointed the light at the casket, then at the blood-spattered wife, and then back at me.

"Johnny? What the heck. What's wrong? Talk to me."

Johnny opened his mouth, but he did not to speak. Instead, he started vomiting all over the central control pedestal and on my right leg.

"For crying out loud." I yelled, while trying to fly the airplane and, at the same time, shield the pedestal with my right hand, given that there were electric buttons on it.

"I'm... I'm, I'm so sorry," Johnny said in tears. "I am not good at seeing blood and witnessing death."

"Shhhhh." I made the universal silence sign, with my puke-covered index finger perpendicular to my lips and pointed back to the woman three times. "Pull your socks up, man. We still have almost four hours to go."

I was covered in a yellowish puke.

"Can you fly the plane while I clean this mess on the pedestal, my hand and my lap?"

Johnny sniffed a couple of times and took the controls of the airplane while I searched for any piece of cloth.

It soon became clear that Johnny would be of no help. Flying at night over that area was flying blind; the cities were so few and far between that the invisible dark horizon obscured all signs of orientation. It was like trying to go downstairs in complete darkness or snowboarding during a whiteout.

As I had my head down, trying to clean the mess with an already grimy piece of cloth that was used to check the engine oil levels, I heard a change of airflow around the airplane. I lifted my eyes to the artificial horizon indicator to see that the airplane had pitched down ten degrees, and was banking 20 degrees to the right.

"You're on a descending spiral." I said a bit exasperated, grabbing the controls back, "My airplane!"

Johnny retracted his hands from the controls right away, much like a cat that accidentally touches cold water.

I gave him the stink eye and then collected my thoughts.

"Wait. Have you had your IFR training yet? Do you know how to fly relying solely on instruments?"

Johnny shook his head.

"Of course not," I reminded myself out loud. "You are not even a private pilot yet. My fault!"

I brought the airplane back to its altitude of eleven thousand feet. After we leveled off, the woman started to wriggle and moan softly at first, then louder and louder.

"Gee... we gotta do something." Johnny said.

"I have an idea. Let's climb to fifteen thousand. She's not used to that altitude, and since this aircraft is not pressurized, the thin air will knock her out."

"Sounds good. Anything from stop her from moaning."

And it sort of worked. By the time I leveled the aircraft at fifteen thousand feet, not only the woman but also Johnny were sound asleep.

Time dragged, seconds felt like minutes and every minute seemed to last for an hour. My eyes were tired of monitoring the airplane's artificial horizon indicator. I knew that there was no impending relief since the autopilot was broken and the copilot was worse than useless. Despite the exhaustion, I briefly lifted my eyes to the Milky Way, glad that despite being moonless, at least the night was clear.

Then, abruptly, the stars also decided to vanish, giving way to a flash of strobe lights reflecting inside the clouds.

That got me by surprise, and a violent updraft tumbled and lifted the aircraft as if it were a made of paper. I knew what was coming in the next seconds, the updraft would give way to a downdraft and we would be in a zero-gravity situation, then sink like an anchor. I barely had time to pull my seatbelt tighter. As predicted, we were weightless for a second and then 'boom!' a downdraft made everything loose shoot up to the top. The casket lifted up and slammed the woman on the airplane's ceiling and then back to the floor. The woman screamed in both panic and pain. Johnny's head also hit the top, waking him up in sheer terror.

"Check on her, check on her." I said, trying to keep the airplane upright.

Johnny grabbed a flashlight and started to position himself when another violent turbulent wave hit. I heard the sound of something hitting the floor.

"Ouch... my head."

"Hold on, hold on. Let's wait for smooth air before we inspect the damage."

"I dropped the flashlight."

"You what? Come on, man?" I said, sweating profusely, while trying to keep the airplane from flipping upside-down.

"She stopped crying." Johnny said.

"That may be good, that may be bad."

"Do you think she's dead?"

"Of course not." I shook my head, "But you will be if you don't find that flashlight now."

In less than a minute we exited the side of a towering cumulus cloud, and even though the air became smooth again, the winds aloft picked up, right on the nose of the aircraft, making me concerned about our capability to reach our alternate airport, if necessary.

Johnny contorted his body until he finally found the flashlight under the copilot's pedals. He climbed between the seats and threw a single flicker of light onto the woman's face.

"Ugh! She's unconscious, but her nose is bleeding badly."

"She hit the ceiling face first."

"How long before we land?"

"A little bit over an hour. I'll start a slow descent as soon as I get contact with Plateau's Princess control tower."

So we did. Thirty-nine minutes to the destination and I established the first contact.

"Joey? Is that you boy?" The veteran tower controller knew me since I was a kid, bugging him in his little tower. Air traffic controllers are extremely tactful professionals; they don't call people by first name over the radio, but the familiar voice gave me relief.

""Yeah, I'm in Papa Tango Echo Bravo India," my official call sign, "And our ETA is 0212, over."

"Roger, buddy, roger. I'll turn on the runway lights by then."

"And Tower... we will need an ambulance; we are carrying a seriously wounded passenger."

141

"OK... I will call for one."

A few minutes later, the tower calls back, "You must be carrying a VIP, uh boy, 'because there are a lot of people waiting for you on the ground, and the ambulance is on its way."

Why does his voice sound different? It's not the same tone I'm used to hearing.

I couldn't help but think.

Or maybe it's me, fatigue and stress messing with my mind.

"You are famous." Johnny said. "Even the controllers know you by your first name."

I allowed a smile of relief. Pretty soon we'd be touching down and the nightmarish mission would be over. Then, sniffing the air, I frowned again.

"Ah, Johnny... did you just... pass gas?"

"Pass what? You mean, fart?"

"Yeah. Can you keep your farts for after we land? If I had a CO_2 alarm here, it would be going crazy."

I didn't, I didn't. I swear... I didn't. Oh... gosh, now I smell it too... did you?"

"No. I asked you, stupid."

Johnny turned the flashlight just in time to see the woman convulsing.

"She is the one passing gas!" I said.

"I think it's worse than just farts." Johnny said.

The foul smell was sickening.

"Disgusting! Open your vents and stick your nose there. We'll be on the ground in thirty minutes."

As we passed nine thousand feet, the skies cleared up completely and could see the city in the distance.

"The town of Plateau's Princess has never looked so beautiful." I said.

"I am going to kiss the ground when we land."

"We should be able to see the airport from here."

"Tower, this is EBI... can you turn the runway lights on?"

No answer.

"Tower, EBI, over."

I looked at Johnny, "What the heck?"

The next voice in the speakers was way too familiar to me.

"Captain, can you hear me?"

It took a fraction of a second to recognize Mr. Zig's voice.

"Mr. Zig? What are you doing in the control tower frequency?"

"Captain... the tower controller cannot turn the lights on. I am here trying to help him. The lights came on and then faded. We don't know what the problem is."

"Is this some kind of a joke?" I said, knowing that Mr. Zig was anything but a prankster. "I'm running low on fuel."

"I wish it was a joke, Captain."

I shook my head in disbelief. We were five minutes from the airport. Johnny's eyes were saucers.

"I'll tell you what, Captain... there are lots of cars at the airport. We can line them on both sides of the runway and you can land."

"I don't know. How long it will take?"

"Ten minutes." Mr. Zig said, "Maybe even less."

"It's a good idea... but I can't take the risk. If we don't land on the first attempt, we'll be toast."

"What are you saying?" Mr. Zig asked.

"I'm saying... if I can't land there in the first attempt, I won't have fuel to reach my alternate, St. Joseph of the Pines."

"It's risky... but I know you can do it!"

I always follow my intuition, and this time it was saying, 'Don't try to be a hero.'

"Forget the cars, boss. I am low on fuel but high on hope. Say a prayer for us. I'm heading to St. Joseph."

After a long pause, Mr. Zig said, "Your decision. We will drive to meet you there... see you in about three hours."

"What the heck are you doing, man?" Johnny firmly grabbed his control wheel as I started heading east, "We won't make it! Look at the fuel gauges. We're gonna die."

"Leave it!" I put my right hand on Johnny's chest and pushed him back, "Do not touch the controls unless I ask you to do so. I'm the pilot-in-command of this aircraft and you have to trust me."

"Well, El Captain." Johnny said in a mordant voice, "If we don't make it, you owe me a life."

St. Joseph's airport was 28 minutes away, and halfway there, we were able to contact the approach controller, who gave us frightening news.

"Echo Bravo India, the airport is still open, but I don't know for how long. Do you have information Foxtrot?"

"We can't get the Automatic Terminal Information Service yet. Could you read it to us?"

"Sure," said the controller, "Wind calm, visibility ½ mile, fog, temperature 6, dew point 6, altimeter 1020. It seems to be getting worse. What is your alternate?"

The airport was operating under instrument conditions and was forecast to close due to fog within the hour. I should have known better, if St. Joseph's airport was famous for anything, it was for its foggy days. The airport was built in an area that was perfect for that meteorological phenomena.

"I don't have one." My voice was weak.

"Say again, EBI."

"Plateau's Princess was my destination. St Joseph of Pines is already my alternate. If we can't land there, any chance to land at the downtown airport, Bacacheri?"

"The downtown airport is operationally closed and even if it was operational, the weather there is even worse. How long can you hold for, EBI?"

"I can't hold."

"What are you saying?" The controller asked.

I sighed and said the words that have the weight of apprehension for every pilot, "Echo Bravo India is declaring an emergency. I am extremely low in fuel. Request vectors for the final approach course."

Terrifying pause, then he came back.

"Understood, Echo Bravo India is declaring an emergency. Fly heading 050, vectors for the final approach course. We will make sure emergency equipment is waiting for you. Say number of souls on board."

I never thought that it would have got to this point.

"Three people aboard. We have a person gravely injured aboard who will need an ambulance right away. We are also carrying a deceased body in a casket."

"You said... an injured passenger and a deceased body?"

"Affirmative. This is a mercy flight."

Another long silence, then, "Roger, three aboard... descend and maintain 6,000 feet."

"I'd like to stay at eight for as long as I can, if it's okay with you."

"Roger that, maintain 8,000. Thirty-two miles to the airport."

Johnny started crying, quietly.

The airport was situated on the east side of a big metropolis. As I approached from the west side, I could see the reflection of the city lights in the lower clouds, giving them the appearance of auburn cauliflowers. I could not see the ground or pinpoint the airport either.

"Echo Bravo India, fly heading 100, descend and maintain 5,000 until the final approach fix, clear ILS runway 15. Contact tower now, 118.15. Good luck."

I read back the instructions to the approach controller and thanked him for his help and good wishes. I was not out of the woods yet; I was hoping to: 1) have enough fuel to complete the approach and, 2) be able to see the runway and land.

"St. Joseph's Tower... this is Seneca Echo Bravo India, six miles out, inbound ILS 15," I said, as calmly as I could as I pressed the push-to-talk button.

"Echo Bravo India, this is St. Joseph's Tower. You are cleared to land runway 15. Emergency equipment in position."

Despite the noise of the engines running, it became eerily silent after I was cleared to land. The woman stopped moaning. And even Johnny stopped crying but made no effort to help me or look for the runway.

I entered the fog about 2,000 feet above the ground. At 500 feet I could hear the echo of my heart inside my headset. At 300 feet, everything below me got a little brighter, 220 feet and I was able to capture a string of strobe lights that lit the entire windshield, the approach light system leading to the airport. At 150 feet, the entire airport was visible.

"Runway in sight." I sighed on the radio.

Right at this point, Johnny removed his head from his lap, or wherever it was, saw the airport and shouted, "We're going to live. We're going to live."

The touchdown was soft, as if it were on butter. I caught a glimpse of emergency trucks as we zoomed by the first half of the runway. I brought the airplane to a complete stop halfway down the runway.

"Great job, Echo Bravo India. Do you want to disembark there or taxi to the terminal?"

"Thanks, tower. I will taxi back to the terminal."

"Turn right on Echo. No need to call Ground. The trucks will follow you. Have a good night."

I taxied the airplane toward the main terminal, being followed by an ambulance and two fire trucks. As soon as I put the parking brake on, Johnny opened the door, jumped off the airplane and kissed the ground even before I was able to bring the fuel levers to the cutoff position and the propellers stopped rotating.

146

The paramedics opened the back door, unloaded the woman and were perplexed to see the makeshift coffin. I completed the after shut-down checklist and before I could exit the airplane myself, two police officers appeared from nowhere, blocked the door and asked, "Do you have a transit permission or death certificate for this body, sir?"

"No, I don't. This is a mercy fl..."

"So, there's nothing I can do but tell you that you are under arrest. Where is the third passenger? We were informed that there were three people on board, and a body."

"What?" I put my hand on my forehead. This was the cherry on top of the cake.

"You have the right to remain silent. Everything that you say may be used against you in court..."

While I was thinking how to explain the situation to the police officer, the corner of my eye caught a shadow crawling under the left wing. It was Johnny running away from our troubles. I couldn't help but laugh at the entire situation. The officers took it as a lack of respect.

Although I was not able to prove my innocence on the spot, I was able to convince the policemen to keep me within the airport area, confined in the airport administrator's office until Mr. Zig arrived.

After an almost three-hour wait, Mr. Zig, my dad and the owner of the trucking company, that employed the deceased driver, arrived in his Crown Victoria Touring sedan. When it became clear that 'a pig's nose was not an electrical outlet' (a popular saying in Brazil to explain a misunderstanding), I was finally released.

I saw the owner of the trucking company talking to the police and then to Mr. Zig. He seemed to be strangely unfazed.

"Sorry for your loss, Sir." I offered my condolences. He simply nodded.

Mr. Zig offered to get hotel rooms for everybody, but all I

wanted was to go home. I would come pick up the airplane and file reports to the aviation authorities, in a few days.

He agreed with my proposal and before I left he asked, "I thought you had a copilot with you?"

"I did… but after the day we had, he became M-I-A."

The four of us got in the car, drove around the airport perimeter for a couple of minutes, looking for Johnny, who definitely didn't want to be found, and then started driving back home, dad and I in the back seat. I fell asleep right away, snoozing for a solid hour. When I woke up, my dad gave me a paternal smile that relaxed me.

"Challenging day at the office, uh, Junior?"

"Yep… it was a marathon, physically and mentally exhausting.

"Well, in the end it was better that you landed in St. Joseph of the Pines. Had you landed in our local airport, things could have got dreadful."

"I know, dad. That's why I didn't want to give them a chance to put the cars beside the runway."

"That's not the reason it could have gotten dreadful, son."
Uh?"

"Do you know who the injured woman really is?"

"The driver's wife… I was told."

Dad shook his head. "Nope. The driver's wife was actually waiting for the body at the local airport. The woman you brought is a prostitute that the driver had picked up, on the side of the road, one day before the accident."

"Say what?"

"Yes, when the word got out that you were bringing another woman, the widow went to the airport to meet her deceased husband and his companion. Her intentions were not good, someone said that she had a knife with her."

I couldn't believe it. Had I landed at the original destination, there would be two dead bodies, instead of one.

The last time I heard about it, the prostitute had survived, but there was a lawsuit to see who was going to pay the medical bills. Since she didn't have money to go back to her original spot, she decided to stay in the big metropolis and became a member of a strip club near St. Joseph's airport.

I never saw Johnny again or found out how he got back to his house. I heard, from other pilots, that he told this story to half of the aviation world, in a completely different version, where he was the ultimate hero for evading the police. He also decided that flying corporate or airlines was not for him and he became a crop-duster pilot and a partner in a mortuary.

As for Mr. Zig... I stayed with him for three years, flying him and his family all over the country, and doing Mercy flights when needed. I've never met a more generous or hard-working person. He believed in my capability more than I was actually capable, and that became a safety problem.

Then, after an engine failure in the middle of a massive squall line, which demanded the use of all my knowledge, skills and good fortune, my guardian angel gave me an ultimatum: "One of us has to look for another job."

I accepted my guardian angel's stipulation and found a safer operation, or else I'm sure you wouldn't be reading this.

CHAPTER EIGHTEEN
The Ditch

In the mid-1990s, Pete Sampras was "the king" on tennis courts, Tonya Harding "the villain" on ice; Bill Clinton lived a sexual harassment nightmare while a South African ex-con was living his dream of becoming president; 'Ace of Base' rocked the top of the Billboard, as Kurt Cobain hit the rock bottom of life; four high school classmates reunited in New York, added two other outliers to the group and a friendship sitcom was born. My sister followed my dad's wish and started law school, while I went to England, on a scholarship, to learn more about the world.

I attended a very diverse college in London, and in my class alone there was a mix of people from five continents, a variety of accents and habits so intricate that it made the learning environment more interesting than the teachers' lectures. Did you know that in Papua New Guinea the ground looks reddish because locals chew the bark of a native ruddy tree and spit everywhere? Or that in some Arab countries people use their left hands to cleanse themselves in the bathroom? I learned that when I tried to shake hands, with a guy from Oman, using my left hand like boy scouts do.

Despite our differences, or thanks to them, the biggest lesson I learned at that time was about the invaluable and timeless attributes of true friendships. It goes above and beyond race, creed,

6666666

We all had the same opinion about Mr. Loyola's English Literature class. It was like waiting in line under a scorching sun listening to the monotone static of a radio for two hours. We even started games like "Incomprehensible Word Bingo" for each time the professor used a word that most of the class didn't understand, and "Yawnucator," for how many times the teacher himself would yawn, bored with his own lecture. The record was 36 times in one hour.

I had gone to England for more reasons than studying English Literature and World War II history. Growing up, while most kids idolized athletes or musicians, I admired a youthful British pilot called David Perrin. He was a member of the renowned Rothmans Aerobatic Team and flew with a perfection that seemed otherworldly. When he tragically perished as a passenger in a helicopter accident, he went from my idol to legend, and I always dreamed about visiting the place he learned to fly, Biggin Hill.

I also had a fascination for the supersonic passenger jet called "Concorde." The double-delta winged airplane that could fly twice as fast as the speed of sound; a trip from London to New York took less than three and a half hours (as opposed to eight hours for other aircraft). Cruising westward at sixty-thousand feet meant that the Concorde arrived before it left. The time zone difference allowed passengers to joke that the jet traveled "faster than the sun." As a matter of fact, the Concorde broke many world records for passenger aircraft, and became such an icon that it starred in one of the Airport movie series "Airport '79."

This fascination for the Concorde led me to bump into a guy from school while attending a small exposition about the jet at Heathrow Airport: Mikko Kovinko, the prototypical Scandinavian lad, paler than a ghost, fair-haired, tall as a skyscraper, as blue-eyed as a Husky and an incredible ineptitude with women. He

AVIATION TALES & TAILS

pronounced English as well as Frankenstein walked.

"Ded yu knaw dat de Concarde arrivas at Heathrow everry Thaarsda arround faive o'clock?"

"Could you repeat that in English, please?"

Mikko didn't think my comment was funny. The tall guy had a tough time with sounds that a different language demanded, but didn't need to be constantly reminded of it.

"Do you mind if I correct your pronunciation every now and then?" I asked him. Finnish pronunciation is rather regular as compared to other languages. As a rule, one letter corresponds to one sound in a fixed manner, and that creates a lot of trouble when trying to learn a multi-sound letter language, like English. For the story's sake, his pronunciation will sound more accurate.

"I'd really appreciate it. I've asked my teachers and host family to correct me, but they never do.

"You got it."

"Anyway, I heard that the Concorde usually lands on runway 35... there's a bus stop close to the threshold... do you want to come and watch it land this Thursday?"

"But I still have a class at that time."

"What class?"

"Professor Loyola."

"Ah, then I'll save you from dying of boredom."

"Have you had...?"

"Yes, I have. Besides, I know from experience that Mr. Loyola doesn't take attendance."

I felt a tad of guilt grabbing at my shoulders as I skipped the last class and entered the double-decker #57 from Kingston to Heathrow; after all I had a scholarship and missing class on purpose felt like bamboozling my good fortune. But the anticipation of seeing the legend live dissolved every hint of shame. After overhearing our intentions, even the bus driver couldn't help but join our conversation.

"You lads heading to Heathrow to see the Concorde, yeah?" Asked the bus driver.

"How did you know?"

"Your cap, mate."

I was wearing an EAA – Oshkosh hat.

"It's a bonnie sight." He continued, "We'll get there about ten minutes before it lands."

"Can you see it well from the bus stop? Do you know if there's a better spot?" Mikko asked.

The bus was not full but the driver gestured for us to get closer, and then said in a whisper, "I don't tell this to many people, but you seem like good chaps..., there is a hole in the bottom of the fence, by the north threshold. About 10 meters inside the fence there's a ditch where the tower's controllers won't be able to spot you, and you'll even feel the jet's blast."

"Hoo-hah. Now we're talking." Mikko slapped me on my chest.

"But if you two get caught, you didn't hear this from me."

"Our lips are sealed." Mikko said.

"By the way, what happens if we are ever caught?" I asked.

"You'll get a warning and have to promise not to do it again."

"That's all?"

"Now, if you're caught twice, your punishment will be more severe."

"Like what?" I asked.

"You'll be forced to drive a London Transit Company bus for the rest of your lives." He winked.

We got there on time and the bus driver wished us good luck. The hole in the fence was not as easy to find as we thought, and we ended up watching the landing from the bus stop. It was quite spectacular anyway. The big jet looked like a hawk descending to catch its prey.

"Look! The nose is being lowered." Mikko pointed out. The

Concorde had a feature that no other airplane had. In the compromise between the need for a streamlined design to reduce drag in flight and the need for the crew to see properly during taxi, takeoff, and landing operations, the pilot could tilt the tip of the aircraft's nose down; this idiosyncrasy was called "droop snoot."

The big jet glided down to earth and we could feel the air pushed aside as it flew over our heads and touched down on the runway with its 10 tires. It made me wonder about the potential of mankind. A little over a century ago, humans didn't know how to fly; now, not only we can fly 10 times the speed of sound, but we've been to the moon and back. What kind of other powers haven't we explored or found yet? Traveling through time? Traveling at the speed of light? At the speed of thought?

Mikko's high modulated voice brought me back from contemplation land, "Let's try to find the hole again."

After spending fifteen minutes inspecting the fence, we found a small gap where we could slide under.

"This is tight. Plus, we are going to get mud on our clothes."

"It will be alright; I'll bring a rubber mat. Are we on for next week?"

"Do Brits like fish & chips?" I answered with a question.

We were expecting to see our fellow bus driver when we boarded the bus the following Friday, but there was another guy behind the wheel. We arrived at the bus stop with plenty of time, slithered our way in and were shocked when a pair of big eyes met ours at ground level.

"Bloody hell! Who the heck are you?" A shaved-head guy whispered loudly at us.

Completely taken aback, we were unable to reply. Then, his hush decreased a bit, "Are you friends with Carlson?"

"Yeah." I managed to utter.

"Oh, then get in 'the ditch,' mates. I'm Jeff." The bald, sharp-nosed man said.

Introductions behind us, Mikko looked at me as to ask, "Who is Carlson?" I made a 'beats me' face and shrugged my shoulders. I was still shaking.

The ditch was as comfortable as a Lazy Boy recliner. Someone had dug it in a way that a person inside the airport grounds looking toward the street could not see it.

"Carl did a good job making this bunker, eh?"

"Sure. I mean, what is this? Some kind of turf-type tall fescue?"

Jeff was glad that I had noticed. "Yeah. He really went above and beyond."

"Where is he today?" I asked casually.

"Oh, I thought he had brought you guys here today? He must be on another route."

By then, we saw the landing lights lining up miles away. The show was about to begin. Tail down, nose up, the bird of metal started getting bigger and bigger until we realized that maybe this wasn't a good idea after all.

"Here we go; get ready, mates."

"Wow... it looks like it is coming straight at us." I said.

Mikko nodded.

"Do you think the pilots can see us, Jeff? And maybe will call the airport police?"

"Aaaah, don't be sissies. It's all a matter of depth and perspective. We can easily see the jet because it's big, but our little bunker is nothing more than a dot for the pilots. By the way, wear green next time." Jeff said.

There was no jet blast, but I was not disappointed. At that point, the jet was crossing our heads about 100 feet from the ground.

"It's some experience, isn't it?" Jeff said with a slap on my back. "I am sure Carl has already advised you to keep it a secret. There are about ten of us that know about the ditch and we don't want the word to spread. If you guys get here and there are already three people in the ditch, back off and watch it from the bus stop. We don't want to raise any suspicion."

We attended the landing every other week and the anticipation got stronger every time. On our fourth time Jeff said, "I won't be coming next week and I don't know where Carl is hiding these days. So, you guys will be the guardians of the ditch."

"Oh, I won't be able to make it either, Jeff. My professor scheduled a quiz right after the last class."

"What about you, Mikko." Jeff asked.

"Maybe; maybe not."

I swear I could see a tiny smirk on Mikko's face and on the way back to Kingston I asked, "So, are you coming alone next Thursday?"

"I don't know yet."

The following week came, and my suspicions grew stronger. On Wednesday I heard some rumors that one of the seniors was taking his classmates to see something amazing. I couldn't find Mikko. Cell phones were not readily available at that time and despite my constant calls, from the infamous British red telephone booths to his host family's house, I could not locate him. On Thursday I ran to the bus station to see if he was going to go, but he was not there either.

When the bus stopped and the door opened, I was greeted with enthusiasm, "Joey! Hop on. Where's Mikko?"

"I am not going today, Carl. I have a Literature test in less than 20 minutes. I just ran here to see if Mikko was going. I have a bad feeling about today."

Carl's face dropped and his voice lowered, "What do you mean?"

"I suspect that Mikko may be planning to take someone else."

"Jeff will be there... he won't let it happen."

"That's the problem... he won't be there. And I won't either; and Mikko knows he is running the show today."

"Listen. I can't hold the bus. And since he's not here, let's hope that those were only rumors. I will have a word with him later."

"So will I, Carl. So will I."

I went back to school and looked for Mikko on the campus before the quiz started, I called his house before and after class. His host dad was starting to get concerned with my calls.

"Is there anything wrong, Joey? Did you have a fight or something?"

"No Mr. Hampton, I just need Mikko to help me with a project." White lie turning grey.

I decided not to think about it anymore.

The big guy would not be so dumb to take other people to our secret, privileged, panoramic site.

But my assumption turned to be correct the next morning. Right when I arrived at school there was gossip going around about some students getting busted.

I saw our lab professor, Mr. Walker walking in large steps across campus and I sprinted to join him, "Professor, professor."

He stopped, slid his glasses to the tip of his nose, and looked at me as if I were a sample to be studied, "Joseph? Yes? How can I help you?"

"People are talking about some students getting in trouble yesterday. Do you know anything about it?"

"Of course. We had a big council meeting this morning; but I am not supposed to talk about it."

"Ah, please tell me, any guys from our class?"

"I am not supposed to discuss the off-campus events that happened yesterday with a student."

"What happened?" I insisted.

The professor looked left and right and said, "Apparently, a

157

bunch of seniors were caught trespassing at Heathrow Airport."

"Oh, how many students?" I gulped. "Who caught them?"

"Four students. A boy and three girls. The airport security caught them. They had made a hole in the fence. How stupid. What were they thinking?"

"Geez! What's going to happen to them?"

"Why are you so interested in this?" Professor Walker asked.

"I think that one of them is a "sort of" friend."

"Sort of dumb friend, you mean."

"Yeah. So, what's going to happen to them?"

"Well, say goodbye to your dumb friend because, as far as I know, all those involved will lose their student visas and will have to leave the school."

The hair on the back of my neck stood up. I felt sick to my stomach.

"Are you OK?"

"Yeah, I am fine. I just can't picture those seniors kicked out of the university."

The professor opened his arms. "C'est la vie! They committed the crime, they have to pay the fine."

I went to class and kept waiting for someone to open the back door and summon me to the principal's office. One word from Mikko and I would be in trouble too. I kept thinking about what would happen to him. He had told me once that his parents were very strict.

One week passed, and I didn't hear anything. All I knew was that the seniors had to return to their respective countries. I talked to Carlson, after the dust settled, and told him what happened. He knew half of it.

"So, that's what they do to foreigners when they catch them?" His tone was too nonchalant. "Better extradition than jail. Jeff is so mad at Mikko for betraying our trust, that if he could put his hands on the chap, there wouldn't be much left. Jeff has vowed to make another hole when things calm down, but I don't think anyone will be willing to share it anymore."

"No problem. I don't think I'd risk getting caught, anyway."

A month later, I got a letter in the mail from Mikko. He apologized for being such a fool and mentioned that his parents had sent him to military school in Finland, a harsh punishment. He ended the letter by telling me that he missed our friendship very much and that he would never forget sharing the Concorde sights together.

I wrote back, thanking him for not dragging me, Carl and Jeff into the mess.

After all these years, we still write sporadic e-mails to each other, like when the movie "Pushing Tin" was released in 1999 (the first and last scenes – when the main characters are flipped in midair by an airplane's wake turbulence - remind us of our adventures) or when the Concorde crashed in Paris on July 25, 2000. It was like the death of a woman that we both had loved. The official investigation concluded that the accident had been caused by a metal part that had fallen from another airplane departing ahead of the Concorde. The metal fragment punctured a tire that exploded and hit the fuel tank. All 109 occupants died. One year after the accident, British Airways and Air France decided to retire the Concorde, alleging passenger uncertainty cumulating with the events of September 11th.

When I was a little kid, I enjoyed sitting beside my grandfather and listening to his pioneering stories. His tales were always filled with first-times, friendships and novelties of bygone days, like when grandpa and his best friend jumped from a water tower into a moving steam engine locomotive, or when his friend (Paolo) took a vulture to a movie theater, concealed under his raincoat, and released the thing during a horror flick. The bird flew straight to the screen and punched a big hole in it.

Now, I can share my stories with the reader, and one of them is about friendship and a big aluminum hawk that descended from the skies to scorch our heads.

I never returned to that bus stop.

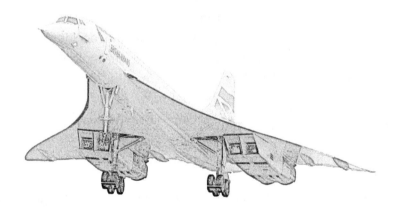

CHAPTER NINETEEN

Hydraulic Dragons

After I graduated, the aviation job market was not showing good signs in Europe, and I elected to go back to Brazil 'on a Wing and a Prayer,' or as Brazilians would say, 'Without a Handkerchief and Without Document.'

Well, not without a document, I had a degree and a license to show, still wondering what the future would hold for me. Except that I did not have to wonder for too long. As soon as I set foot in the country, a friend was waiting for me at the airport and asked if I would be interested in getting his position, as he was moving to bigger and better things. I took the job even before I could find a place to live.

Except that, after experiencing the comfort and safety of flying abroad, the risks involved with flying in Brazil became a disturbing nuisance, every so often trying to destroy life.

So, I jumped from one corporate job to another, then to another. until I was finally able to get to the airlines; but, with the airlines came "The Dragons."

"It's all set, Joey. Ground school for two weeks and then you start simulator training on the twenty-fourth," said the Director of Operations of the airline.

"What kind of simulator is it?"

"Ah, it's a Level D Full Motion Flight Simulator," he said with much pride.

The only flight simulator I had ever trained on were the ones that can run on a personal computer, and the good old Frasca static flight simulators.

If you have never been to a facility where they have a real simulator, or as I call it, the Dragons' Den, let me describe my first introduction to it. The hotel van dropped me off in front of a building that lacked any personality. It was a giant box-like structure, dull as cement. The few tiny windows were dark in a way that indicated that the sun would not stand a chance, the walls were painted in a kind of shade that had been outcast from the brown family and was not accepted by the grey family either.

Dreadful! was my first thought, *Fire the architect.*

Later on, I came to learn that all Dragons' Dens were like that because of the need to run hydraulic lines and keep the simulators cool.

I was led to a mockup classroom with internal windows that offered a view of the metallic creatures. Monstrous flight simulators lined up, one after another, ready to eat their prey. Well, at the time I didn't know I would be having such feelings about them. Everything was new and interesting to me.

But one could not help noticing the constant jerky movements of the flight simulators with student pilots that would arrive with a smile, but would exit as if they had just wrestled a grizzly bear.

We were a class of eight guys, and had one ground instructor (Hanger), an ex-marine who enjoyed giving military nicknames to the ones that didn't already have one. Hanger's real name was Clifford Hook.

Upon hearing the news about our nicknames, an excited redhead kid lifted his hand and asked, "Can I be Maverick?"

"Sure, Freckles. Anybody else want to be Maverick?"

Dead silence.

"Okay... if any of you guys were in the military, write your nickname in big letters on this paper, fold it and leave where we can all see it... if you were not military, I already have your names based on your profile.

Our line-up turned out to be: **Freckles** (the wannabe Maverick); **Sprinkles** (a guy that was so addicted to the candy that his tongue was permanently colorful), **Diaper** (not for the reasons you may think – when he was a kid, the big guy called the constellation that looks like a bowl and a handle, by the wrong name – for his own luck, he became "Big D" with time), **Scooby** (whose voice reminded everyone of the cartoon character – I wonder what ATC thought about it, every time he spoke on the radio), **Trojan** (he said it was his military nickname – never proved why), **Milagro** (there's always a religious one), **Duster** (an ex Ag-pilot) and me (**Beefsteak** – not easy to be a vegetarian in a carnivore world).

Every time one of the simulators made a furious noise and dropped violently, in plain view, we would look at each other with fear spitting from our stomachs to our nostrils; but those nervous looks actually made me feel less anxious – I was not alone with my fears.

Hanger would look at us and, with a smile that made me uneasy, he would say, "Don't worry... your time will come."

Your time will come. That phrase has never been said while foreseeing a good outcome.

Only one of the guys (Trojan) had been in a flight simulator, and when questioned by the others, he would brag and play tough guy, "What kind of pilots are you guys? Scared of a flight simulator."

"Every time I look at them, 'the Imperial March' starts playing in my head," said Freckles.

"What's the Imperial March?" asked Duster.

I looked at him as if he had been living under a rock, "Darth Vader's theme."

163

Skittles, the most levelheaded guy in class and our elected philosopher, calmly opened another pack of the sugary stuff and said, "I'm not as afraid of the machine as I am of the unknown."

When the time finally came, I was glad to be paired with Skittles in the simulator, even though he was paler than me during the briefing.

Martin, a Kentucky-born flight instructor assigned to us, didn't make our life any easier with his accent and rapid-fire speech. We felt as if he talked with no spaces between the words.

"Yafolksreadyfursomedoomandgloom?"

I looked at Skittles, who looked back to me, twisting his lower left lips, discreetly shaking his shoulders.

"Dedthacatetayallstongue?"

"We are good, Sir." I answer the way Hanger liked.

We got into the heart of the dragon, which looked just like the aircraft we were going to fly, and things were good until the beast awoke. I got sick after 30 minutes in it, but it was nothing like motion sickness, it was a feeling that I understood only after years of research. Apparently, I was one of a very small percentage of pilots who have highly acute vision. My eyes would perceive discrepancies between the virtual reality screens and what my brain deemed as expectable and acceptable. It can cause havoc in ones' head, notwithstanding whether the simulator is in motion or not. The main symptom is a major migraine that has as sub-symptoms: discomfort, disorientation and nausea.

Martin had to stop the session several times, so that I could gain some composure.

I exited the end of the first sim session looking like I had been run over by a train. Duster and Scooby, who were going to start their session after us, were horrified by the way I looked.

"Nevaseensomndyfeelthesbad," said Martin. "Take someds morrow."

By "someds," Martin meant motion sickness medicine. Which I did take, and did learn that they made things even worse; not only they were ineffective for my symptoms, but they also made me drowsy.

Years of doing aerobatics and going to amusement parks, I knew that I didn't suffer from motion sickness. I knew that it was not the motion itself that caused the migraine. We even tried an entire session without the motion, with the same results. The microsecond difference between what the instruments were telling me, what the airplane should be doing and what the screen was reproducing, caused a mess in my brain. It was even worse on the simulated ground, during taxi or simulated repositions.

The synthetic environment was not as close to reality as my senses wanted, creating a conflict between my visual and vestibular receptors, which led to my brain rejecting the information needed to maintain orientation.

Day after day, Skittles had to almost carry me back to my room, sit me on my bed and hear me crying that my aviation career was over.

"Don't say that! It's not over."

"How can it not be, if I cannot fly the freaking simulator? It's not an airplane! It's nothing more than a glorified video game."

I had never been a fan of video games. During my adolescence, while my friends were indoors, mastering Atari joysticks, I was outdoors, trying crazy maneuvers on my BMX bike.

"You just have to deliberately fight the pain."

"I can't even taxi the thing on the virtual ground, Ski."

"You cannot give up, Steak. Not now, not ever."

If it weren't for Skittles, I would have packed my bags and left after the second day in the simulator. He made me fight every day.

Not only did I have to concentrate on not getting sick (to a point that I could barely function) but I also had to deal with the

165

training and all the simulated emergencies that were thrown at me.

The advantage of a flight simulator is that you can lose engines, have a major fire aboard, get iced up to the point of becoming an airborne popsicle, suffer landing gear malfunctions and have electrical, hydraulic and pneumatic issues without the end result being tainted by blood, pieces of flesh and airplane parts scattered about. In the worst-case scenario, all one could get, in a series of wrong decisions during an emergency, was a red screen and a 'do over' remark. Well, that's what I thought.

Thanks to Skittles, I passed my training and accepted the fact that I would have to suffer that type of torture twice a year, in order to keep doing the job I loved doing.

And, for me, that fact made the real emergencies, in real airplanes, much less challenging.

I learned two valuable lessons in flight simulators though, which I could not have learned anywhere else.

First lesson: Hindsight is 20/20, so don't judge!

When I was flying for a cargo company, one of our guys, who I did not know personally, flew into a mountain right after takeoff; it was almost a poster case for CFIT (Controlled Fight into Terrain). The accident happened at night during a snow shower and, as happens with any aviation accident, there was a lot of speculation. It did not take long for people to start pointing fingers, and I fell for that fallacy too.

How could an experienced pilot, who had been flying that route for many years, make such a disastrous mistake?

Two months passed, people stopped talking much about the accident, and it was time for me to go to my 6-month simulator torture. On the first session, without any advanced notice, my instructor configured my departure to be from the airport my coworker had had the accident, during the same time of the day and same weather conditions.

166

Even though I was devoting 50% of my attention to not getting sick in the simulator, the other 50% started suspecting that the instructor was up to something, but I didn't connect the dots.

"Why are we flying from this location? We normally fly the New York or Memphis scenarios on the first day." I casually asked the instructor.

"Just a change of scenery." He replied as nonchalantly.

I knew that something was about to happen. Something bad always happens in simulator sessions.

For some reason, the setting felt oddly familiar.

I took off, followed the standard instrument departure procedure, and all of a sudden aural warnings and master caution lights that should not be displayed together, turned the cockpit into a 1990's rave.

That's when the human factor enters the stage. I knew the airplane very well, and acknowledged the fact that some lights and sounds mixing in front of me made no sense whatsoever. Precious seconds passed before I concluded that there were no *memory items* for this situation, and I should grab the Quick Reference Handbook and try and figure out what was going on. I looked down to the right to grab the book, and was startled by another warning in the middle of all the warnings: **"Whoop, whoop. Terrain, Terrain... pull up, pull up."**

"What?"

I looked up to my lights first and then to the screen. And the simulator came to a strong halt, the sound of crash and a red screen.

"You're dead." I heard from the back.

Just like the pilot who became a real casualty in the accident, I broke the fundamental laws in an emergency: Aviate, Navigate & Communicate. When the problem arose, I continued flying the aircraft, but abandoned my situation awareness; and since everything was pointing to an electrical failure, I decided not to rely on the autopilot. My plate became so full that food fell on the ground.

"How is it possible? These lights should not appear in flight."

"If it is of any solace... eleven out of twelve pilots, in the last month alone, did exactly the same thing."

"Is this what really happened in that flight?"

"Uh-huh."

The instructor explained the ridiculous scenario that led those lights and warnings to appear together. It seemed that no one had ever thought it could happen; maybe that's why it did.

I felt a mix of embarrassment and shamefulness. How easy it is to be sympathetic when it's ourselves we see in the line of fire.

<u>Second Lesson</u>: Never say never.

Much of a pilot's simulator experience depends on the type of instructor one gets (mainly for pilots who struggle with the fake visuals). Most of time you get instructors that are understanding, and without making any concessions, they make your ride less excruciating; but there are always exceptions to the rule. A decade or so ago, I got a sim instructor who could care less for my well-being inside "the box." It is not that he made my life miserable on purpose, but did nothing to ease the tussle. For instance, when sim instructors reposition the aircraft, most will say, "Look down, look somewhere else, close your eyes, just don't look at the screens." The instructor I got, at that time, didn't do that. He would play with repositioning without giving me a heads up, which gave me an even more distressing headache.

When the training part was done, I was hoping to get a more empathetic check airman. Nope, that did not happen. The caring ones must have been on vacation that week. The proficiency check consisted of a one-hour oral, followed by a two-hour checkride. I remember looking at the sim clock when I walked in: 11:47 PM. The ride was so demanding that I walked out drenched in sweat, with a pounding headache so fierce that I was not able to read the time on the clock, it was all a big blur.

The check airman gave me my paperwork, sort of congratu-lated me and disappeared in a maze of doors and aisles.

I walked out of the square ash-grey building and felt the heavy air of autumn. It was past 2 o'clock in the morning and there was no one around. I needed to compose myself first, so I sat down on the curb before walking the one and a half miles that separated the simulator facilities from the hotel.

As I sat there, I stared at the building and deliberated.

You repulse me. I know you are a necessary evil and that I should be thankful for my job that provides this type of training, but that doesn't automatically mean I have to show you any def-erence. At least you can't physically kill me, but you cause me tremendous agony.

I stood up and started walking back to the hotel, promising myself to not even look at the building on the way to the airport, later on.

It was around 09:50 AM when I was awakened by a loud boom that almost threw me off the bed.

"What the heck?!"

It felt as if two semis had crashed head-on in front of the hotel. I opened the window but could not see anything from my side. I opened the door to see other startled guests by a window, over-looking south, toward the airport. As I put my pants on and went to join them, I heard sirens.

"What is it?" I asked anyone, before getting to the window.

"An airplane has just crashed."

"At the airport?"

"Looks like," someone said.

It was within the airport property, alright, more precisely in the building I had occupied less than eight hours before. A twin tur-boprop lost one engine right after takeoff, stalled and spun to the ground, hitting the building which hosted many flight simulators.

The crash killed the pilot (the only occupant of the aircraft) plus three people on the ground, who were trapped in the same flight simulator I had been in earlier that morning.

On my way to the main terminal, my hotel van driver had to take a different route, because the road in front of the flight simulator building was closed.

From afar, I could see that smoke was still coming from what was once a structure that I despised. I felt sorry for the pilots that perished in the accident and for their families. A fatidic coincidence.

It could have been me.

CHAPTER TWENTY

Towering Memories

On a similar story involving everlasting memories, most of us can share one that has changed not only the future of aviation but also that of the humankind.

If I ask you, "Where were you when…" you would not hesitate giving me a detailed description of that fatidic morning, maybe even remembering what you had for breakfast or the exact clothes you were wearing.

My daughter had been born twenty days earlier, and I had not been able to get much sleep since her birth. I checked in with my dispatcher around 04:20 AM PST, and he told me that the trunk airplane would be thirty minutes late to arrive at my base airport. That kind of holdup always caused a domino effect throughout the system and was a nuisance to everyone involved, but on that morning, I was thankful for the delay because it would allow me to stretch out on my cargo airplane seats, and sleep for at least twenty-five minutes.

I opened the cargo doors, pre-flighted the bird, went to the pilots' room to check my flight plan, the weather and NOTAMs. The other pilots arrived as I was leaving the room to nap in the airplane.

"Where are you going?" Someone asked me.

"He looks like a zombie," I remember our base commander

replying for me, "He is probably heading back to the airplane, where it's quieter. Let the boy catch some sleep."

We had an amazing group of pilots who supported each other. They had created a pool, betting on the day my daughter would be born. The winner shared the prize with me, and I invested it in treasury bonds. To celebrate the occasion, I handed out cigars to them. I think the only disappointment was that the cigars were made of chocolate, and they were hoping for real ones, maybe from Cuba.

I got into the cockpit, pulled both seats close to the panel and reclined the seats as much as I could; then, I assumed the position of a veteran contortionist and fell asleep like a rock (I don't know where the expression, "sleeping like a baby" originated. My baby did everything but sleep). I was immersed in some dreamland when someone knocked hard on the side of my airplane. I completely ignored it, I thought it was someone trying to scare me; but then, the knocks persisted, and I opened the side window and saw that it was Sanders, one of our pilots.

"What?" I grumpily said, with just one eye opened.

"Lock and secure all the airplane doors and come to the pilots' room right now. We're being attacked."

"Uh? What the fudge?" Still in sleepy daze, I didn't pay much attention to him. After all, Sanders was one of the victims of my pranks, and I thought he was getting payback.

Still with one eye opened, I checked my watch; it was 05:51 AM PST. I lifted my head over the panel just enough to see if the trunk airplane had arrived yet. As it hadn't, I closed my eye.

A few minutes later, another knock. This time, it was our base commander, "Joey… lock the airplane NOW! And come to the pilots' room.

Cheeses! What does a pilot have to do to get some sleep here?

172

While locking the aircraft, I noticed that not only the trunk air-plane hadn't arrived, but there was not a single soul at the al-ways-busy ramp.

Strange.

For the first time, "We're being attacked," started to sink in, and I ran to the pilots' room, where a crowd was facing the TV.

I walked in and before I could vocalize, "What's going on?" the second airplane hit the south tower.

A dismal "Oooooooooooooh," filled the room, replacing the air of everyone's lungs.

I leaned against the wall, not to fall. It could not be real.

The first thought that popped in my mind was the people that were in the airplane and those in the towers. The second, the safety of my loved ones.

Soon after, came the news about the attack on the Pentagon.

What's next? Who's next?

We just stood there, speechless, defenseless, fish in a barrel, ready to be snatched.

Word came that the entire U.S. airspace was closed until fur-ther notice, and "further notice" could mean hours, days, even weeks.

Then, the towers collapsed, sinking with it the souls of an en-tire world. It looked like one of those planned demolition events, but this time, there were people trapped inside, and brave people trying to save them.

About an hour later, the station manager told us to go home and "hug your loved ones."

The drive home was surrounded by such surrealism that even the hope of everything being a nightmare was unacceptable. Most people felt instantly sorry for the people in the airplanes and twin towers; but as a pilot, I could not stop thinking about my aviation colleagues that were in charge of the flights, before evil took over. And then, the fact that it was on our soil.

Was this the way people felt during the attack on Pearl Harbor?

I got home, hugged and cried with my family, as most people did. The sky was clear, but the day was dark. After the relief of being with my family, a vindictive feeling took over. All I wanted was for the accountable criminals to be caught and receive their punishment.

The silence from the lack of airplanes in the sky had permeated the air. It felt as if even the birds refused to fly. People stayed in their homes, like soldiers in a bunker, waiting for the enemy to either attack or retreat.

Wednesday came, and with it, the assertion that it had not been a bad dream. The news searched for answers and 'what ifs,' while replaying the scenes over and over.

Thursday morning, I got a call from my flight follower. He told me I would be the first flight out of our local airport, and probably the first civilian flight out of northern California.

"Are you okay with it?"

Without knowing what else to say, I just replied, "Yes."

He gave me precise instructions to comply with, the short list of people I could talk to. I arrived at the dead airport at noon and was met by the security people I had been briefed about. It almost felt like a secret service operation.

It was so nice to be able to be in the air and talk to an air traffic controller. From the air, everything looked the same, but for humankind, everything had changed. They had used airplanes as weapons. The word "hijack" would never again be described as a way for someone to force an airliner to land in a different country to request asylum.

After passing my third fix, literally out of the blue, the voice of ATC came through my headset as calm as the ocean breeze.

"You will have company at your nine o'clock in about 30 seconds. You know what to do."

Before I could let my "Uh?" show him my confusion, a F-16 approached on my lower left, the pilot struggling to slow his jet to my cruise speed. I had the emergency frequency on COMM 2 and checked in with him.

The pilot's head turned toward me, he called my call sign, "… is everything okay?" He asked as he passed my aircraft.

Mesmerized by the beauty and incongruity of it all, I only managed to reply, "Affirmative."

He made a wide left turn, and repositioned himself again on my left side for a last time before making a hard left and disappearing from view.

From that point on, I knew we would rebound, I knew that we would be more than okay, and even though we could not erase that brutal past, justice would be served. Yet, to this day, it is still heart-wrenching to watch reruns of my favorite sitcom (F*R*I*E*N*D*S) that were shot prior to that date, showing the towers sitting omnipotent, a symbol of human progression and sovereignty.

CHAPTER TWENTY-ONE
Communic-action

One of the aviation gems I've learned throughout the years is that unless you are going to hit a mountain, there's no point in arguing with an Air Traffic Controller over the radio. It's like arguing with a referee in the middle of a match, or the old maxim about wrestling with a pig.

The first reason not to do so is based on the simple fact that air traffic controllers are highly trained professionals whose primary function is safety. In other words, they are there to add to air safety, and not to be your servant nor to make your life miserable (well, if you pester them enough... maybe). Secondly, they have 'the big picture' right in front of their eyes, and can't simply sit back and let you do whatever you want to do or just witness traffic develop by itself. If that were the case, our world would be filled with violations, resolution advisories and midair collisions. The last reason had to do with the doctrine that started as Cockpit Resource Management, then turned into Crew Resource Management (although I think we should drop the "C" and evolve to an "A" as in Aviation Resource Management), because we depend on each other for a positive outcome.

But pilots still say unthinkable things over the radio, either on purpose or by accident. We also make the controllers repeat themselves (because we are not paying attention), we forget to push buttons and end up making inflight lengthy speeches in ATC frequencies, clogging them; and most prominently, some pilots MEOW on the Emergency (Guard) Frequency.

For instance, I once flew with a pilot who got irritated when the clearance controller gave him a squawk code 6666.

"SAY AGAIN, the code."

The controller patiently and unpretentiously repeated the code, just to be met with a "You gotta be kidding me, right? What do you think we are?"

I was as shocked with the reaction of my cockpit partner as the controller in the tower probably had been.

"Sorry, sir. These codes are computer generated. If you want, I can request another one."

"OF COURSE, WE WANT ANOTHER ONE." Rudeness in form of a person.

"That'll be just a second." Replied an apologetic controller.

We? Oh, heck no, keep me out of your rants.

"Are we 'very superstitious,' here?" My right eyebrow completely raised. By his stance, I knew he was not joking.

"This is b*** s***, man. They cannot treat us like that."

"I, personally, can't see any harm with that squawk."

"Are you taking his side?"

"Nope... I am taking common sense's side."

Weird silence... the corrosive of CRM.

And that's how the flight ended up late, we were sequenced behind several aircraft for departure. One might think it was just a coincidence.

A week after the occurrence, I talked to the controller and apologized for my coworker's behavior. He told me that he and his coworkers felt sorry for the pilot who had to fly with that dude.

Some pilots think that they are really sharp on the radio, but controllers are more quick-witted. There's the classic scene of an aircraft that was cleared for takeoff and spotted a dog on the runway.

"Flight 98, you are cleared for takeoff."

"Ah... tower, Flight 98... there's a dog on the runway."

"Roger that. Flight 98, hold your position. Dog... you are cleared for takeoff."

My best personal ATC experience was abroad.

It was one of those murky winter mornings in South America. We were ready to start engines and get the 'heckoutofthere!' (feel free to substitute the first two letters of the exclamation with something more R-rated), but the fog was so thick that if you splashed cold raspberry extract up in the air, you could have slushy before it hit the ground (the visibility was about 1/8 of a mile - no RVR readings, of course - and the airport required 1/2 mile for takeoffs and landings).

B-O-R-I-N-G!!! I was monitoring the radio for any weather changes, just like watching paint drying on the wall, while daydreaming about a real clean bed and summertime.

The faint radio static was so white-noisy that it put me in a trance; but then, all of a sudden, I heard this guy coming strong, speaking in the local language with authority (CC – Closed Captioning brought to you by my unwillingness to write both languages):

"Ground Control, this is Snakehead 74... ready to taxi with Kilo."

Snakehead 74? I thought to myself, *That's such a cool call sign... I wish I could see what kind of plane this dude's flying.*

"Snakehead 74. This is Ground. The field is closed for takeoffs and landings, due to fog."

I felt the controller wanted to add "Duh?!" at the end of his transmission, but didn't.

"Roger that, Ground." The pilot said with a humph... like, 'Can't you see that I know that?' then added, "I would like to taxi to runway 12 anyway, and be ready to depart as soon as it gets better."

"Roger, Snakehead... like yesterday, it may take a while for this fog to lift, though."

"Ground... Snakehead 74 still wants to taxi to runway 12."

Long pause... then, "Affirmative. Snakehead 74, cleared to taxi to runway 12 via Charlie, Foxtrot, Lima, you can hold short of runway 12 and either stay with this frequency or switch to tower. I am managing both frequencies."

Snakehead 74 read back and started his taxi. I heard the noise of his engines as he passed by us, but the fog was still so thick that one couldn't see anything.

I switched to the tower frequency on our number 2 radio, thinking 'if this guy gets to take off now, there will be a rush to start.' There were at least 10 planes ready to leave.

After 20 minutes, as I was wondering about the amount of fuel the pilot was burning, in whatever fighter jet he was flying, he called tower:

"Tower... Snakehead 74 ready for take-off."

Tower answers right away, "Snakehead 74, hold your position, no changes in the weather."

Another 10 minutes dragged, and Snakehead tried again, getting the same answer.

Add another 8 minutes and the pilot stated with full weight, "Tower... Snakehead 74, it looks much better from where I am sitting, and I am ready for take-off, NOW!"

That was not enough to deeply impress the tower/ground controller, who at this point had probably recorded his negative reply and was just pushing his buttons.

Many of the ATC in South America are military personnel, so after another 3 minutes, Snakehead decided that it was time to show who was in charge.

179

"Tower, Snakehead 74... This time, I am not asking your authorization. This is Lieutenant Colonel Francisco Vispatti informing YOU that I am departing runway 12, NOW."

Pause on the radio. I knew all the pilots were listening to this exchange... it went from drama to comedy to suspense. We couldn't wait for what was coming next.

"Is this departure a matter of national emergency?" Asked the cool, calm and composed under-ranked controller.

"Negative," replied the Lt. Col.

Brief tense pause, and then, as he pressed the mike, one could almost feel the smile in the controller's voice, "Roger! In that case... Snakehead 74, continue holding your position... Lieutenant Colonel Francisco Vispatti... YOU, Sir, are cleared for take-off."

By clearing the person - not the aircraft - for take-off, the controller got a standing ovation from all the pilots listening on the radio. That was the only time I have ever heard clapping and whistling over the radio.

Short story long, the Lt. Col. did not dare to take off without a clearance, and the controller was probably court-martialed the next day, but, boy... the guy had guts.

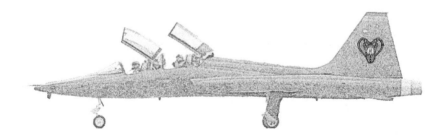

CHAPTER TWENTY-TWO

Christmas Casualty

Since the practice of online shopping was introduced in the mid-1990s, there's no more stressful time in the life of a cargo pilot (a.k.a. freight dog) than the weeks preceding Christmas. It is complete chaos, cargo companies hire a bunch of temporary workers with no experience (ramp loaders, logistic personal and truck drivers) but no extra seasonal pilots.

In the company I worked for, no pilot could take vacation from the third week of November until the end of the first week of January. Despite all the commotion, the distribution always looked like a work of art in action. The widebody jets arrived at the main hubs from the main headquarters, the freight got unloaded, sorted out and loaded in small turboprops that would serve towns with short-runway airports.

It was December 22nd of early 2000s, and I was on the second leg of an eight-leg day, hauling packages all over California. I was already running late because our trunk flight from Memphis had arrived late at our base hub.

Before the first flight of each day, we had a briefing that included the weather and other essential information pertaining to the flights. On that particular day, the weather forecast for my second airport was not encouraging, so I asked to have my airplane filled with as much fuel as I could carry, taking the cargo loads in consideration.

The flight to the first destination was easy and uneventful, but as predicted, when I arrived at my second destination, an airport I prefer not to identify, the weather had gone from bad to worse, and there were already two airplanes holding on the final approach fix, waiting for the visibility to increase and to receive an approach clearance.

"Pack 8650, what are your intentions?" The NorCal Air Traffic Controller wanted to know if I was going to hold or go to the alternate airport in my flight plan. The small airport didn't have a control tower, and instrument approaches were sequenced in accordance to the NorCal Air Traffic Control. When cleared for the approach, pilots would switch frequencies and report their position to a local frequency, letting the airplanes around the airport know their positions. After landing, you had to call center and close your flight plan.

I pressed the push-to-talk button on my control wheel and said, "I will have to hold... request holding at 10,000 feet, right turns and 10-mile legs."

I considered going to my third destination, but at the same time I knew how desperate my ground crew was to get their freight, and they kept reminding me on the company frequency, "Joey... how does it look from up there? From the ground it looks like it is getting better."

"Really? Can you see the lamppost across the runway, in front of the hangar?"

"No."

"So, stop calling me until you see it... because that will mean the visibility is at least ¼ of a mile."

As time passed by, the airplanes below me kept asking for updates from ATC every five minutes, making the controller a bit more than annoyed, "No... the weather is STILL down, it is exactly what the Automated Surface Observing System is reporting."

Ten minutes later, the pilot of the first airplane in line for the approach called the air traffic controller to report that he would have to go to his alternate airport, 50 miles down the road, for fuel. And the controller cleared him to head that way.

No more than 5 minutes later, the pilot of the second airplane in line, maybe influenced by the decision of the first, reported that he would need to do the same.

Given that I had lots of fuel in my tanks, I became first in line.

Another 15 minutes passed, and while I was debating with myself what was going to give in first, the weather or my bladder, my ground crew called me to say that they could see the lamp-post across the runway. I called the controller and he reported that the weather was improving, and I could get an approach clearance within a few minutes.

An approach clearance was exactly what it says, it is a clearance to shoot an approach, but it doesn't guarantee that the pilot will be able to see the runway and land.

I called my ground crew and told them that if everything went well, I'd be on the ground within another 10 minutes. They told me that they couldn't wait to see me (meaning, the cargo). But what they failed to communicate to me was the fact that there were around two thousand kids on the airport ramp, anxiously waiting for an airplane that was bringing Santa Claus to kick off the Christmas weekend of festivities in the city. That airplane was the one that was second in line, when I arrived.

That was the first failure in communication.

The second exchange fiasco was a byproduct of the first. Since I didn't know that there was an airplane carrying Santa Claus, I didn't tell my ground crew that Santa's pilot had decided to go to another city to get fuel; and nobody informed the poor four adult chaperones that Santa Claus' airplane had left the premises and would return later, when the weather was better.

By the time I was cleared for the approach, the weather had

improved even more, to the point that the visibility had increased to almost one mile. Still, it was a tight approach and I was glad to see the approach landing lights and the runway.

The touchdown occurred as expected, and as I rolled out I called the NorCal approach controller to report that I was on the ground and that flight plan could be closed.

As I exited the runway and turned onto the taxiway leading to my ramp, my left eye caught a glimpse that could only be a figment of my imagination: a stampede of kids heading toward my airplane.

This cannot be happening.

Then, a voice on the radio verified what was too surreal to be true.

"JOEY! JOEY! A bunch of kids are running to meet your airplane. They think you are the airplane carrying Santa Claus." It was my ground crew, warning me, almost too late.

"What the heck!" I said out loud.

I slammed on the brakes, grabbing the fuel shutoff lever and bringing it to cutoff right away, knowing that the propeller blades of my turboprop were going to slice a couple of kids if I didn't act pronto.

In less than ten seconds, as the turbine spooled down, my airplane was surrounded by a sea of kids, jumping and screaming, "SANTA CLAUS! SANTA CLAUS!"

Fed up with the situation, I opened my door, stuck half of my body outside and shouted, "KIDS, KIDS..."

They looked at me waiting for a big announcement, or for Santa to jump off the airplane.

I don't know what got into me, maybe it was the stress caused by the rush, but I had to get rid of those kids and, without missing a beat, I said out loud, "...this airplane **is not** carrying Santa Claus. There was an accident with Santa Claus' airplane ten miles north. Santa Claus died, the Easter Bunny died and the

Tooth Fairy died. They all died."

Now, eerie silence for three seconds and then the floods of tears started, right at the time the chaperones arrived at the airplane. The crying was even more deafening that the screaming of joys had been.

The chaperones were astounded, they looked at me, "What did you tell them?"

One kid pulled one of the chaperone's arm and uttered between sobs, "Santa Claus is dead."

He looked at me, lasers coming from his eyes.

I shrugged my shoulders and pointed to my ground crew's hangar, "Can you, please, get the kids out of here? I have to get to the ramp, NOW!"

The chaperones moved the herd of tearful children away. I made sure that there were no strays around the props, started the engine and was finally able to taxi to the hangar.

The aircraft marshaller taxied me in, and as soon as I properly shut down the engine, he run toward my cockpit, "Joey... we thought we were going to witness a carnage. If you hadn't stopped and shut off the engine on time, you would have killed a bunch of children."

I nodded, still a bit shocked, not sure if it was from the fact that I almost had a kid strike or because of my words to the children.

"Why are they all crying now? Did they realize you were not the airplane carrying Santa? What did you say to them?"

"Guys, GUYS... too many questions. Unload your stuff because I have six more legs to go." I was more in disarray than the ramp personal, and all I wanted was to get out of there.

Freight unloaded, I took off from the small-town airport and carried on my day as if nothing had happened, waiting for a management phone call that I knew was coming.

The call I was dreading didn't come that day or any other day.

But, the next day, I did get a call from one of the ramp guys, who told me that I was famous.

"What do you mean, 'famous'?"

"You made it in the city newspaper!"

"Oh no! What does it say?"

"Don't worry. It does not mention your name."

"For goodness sakes. What does it say?"

"The headline says, 'Cargo pilot ruins Christmas in (the city name).' And then it continues with a chaperone quoting what you said to the kids. Is that true? The Easter Bunny and Tooth Fairy too?"

"Ah... I don't know, maybe." I mumbled on my side of the line, waiting for his judgment.

"Man... that was comically tragic. You're a genius."

"Did Santa's airplane finally make it to the city?"

"Yeah... one hour after you left. Some kids had already gone home."

"Oh man. I feel terrible."

"It was not your fault they only had four chaperones and could not control the herd."

"Can you do me a favor?"

"Sure. For you, anything. You're the man!"

"Please ask the guys not to mention my name, about the story."

"No worries. You are our hero. Santa Claus' dead." You know how many kids will need to visit a therapist because of your quick thinking?"

"I am not proud."

I could hear him laughing as he hung up the phone.

I think that by this time, I won't get that dreaded phone call anymore. But, since then, I have been on top of the Santa Claus' naughty list, got a couple of rotten eggs for Easter and my dental plan deductible has increased three times.

CHAPTER TWENTY-THREE

Be Among the Best

The only reason a person may not think that the grass is greener on the other side is if one is colorblind. It's a natural tendency for us humans to compare ourselves to others, and unless you are really satisfied with what you have, you'll always believe that someone else has it better than you.

If someone asked what my dream job would look like, I would describe a job that gives me the freedom to hand fly a jet aircraft, as well as having the capability to use all the available technology; a job where I enjoy the companion of every coworker, a job that pays me decently (enough to recognize my skills, but not so much that would make me feel I didn't deserve the compensation), a job where I could learn with people that were much better than me and could contribute to its unique melting pot, a flying job that brings me home every day and would allow me to sleep in my own bed every night, a job where 'Safety #1' was not a fading poster behind an office door, but a constant undertaking; a job where I didn't have to work weekends or holidays, a job where the pursuit of perfection was a daily goal, and a job that would give me the most precious thing in the world: time. Time to spend with family and friends, time to live life to the fullest and be helpful, time to write a book about the right and wrong choices that brought me here.

The person asking would shake their head while laughing and say, "That job, my friend, doesn't exist. But, hey, one can dream."

As I mentioned in one of the chapters above, that's an easy answer. To give up, to abandon one's dreams, to satisfy yourself with a lukewarm, numb life. But do you really want to get to the end of this life and pose the regretful question, 'What if?'

I knew the job existed. Someone, some company had to have such values.

If it is out there, I will find it.

When I had that thought, I had no idea that not only did it exist, but it was also within 'my arms reach.'. It took years of research and putting the idea on the back burner until the day I heard someone checking in with Seattle Center, in a melodious voice, "Seattle Center, good morning, High Sky three five seventy-six, leaving two three zero to flight level three six zero."

Who on earth (or sky) is High Sky?

In any circle of professional aviators, there's always a pilot who is the Encyclopedia Britannica of Aeronautics, someone that actually knows a lot of data and facts. In my cargo company, that guy was Kevin. He always arrived at our final destination 15 minutes before I did.

"Kevin, Kevin!" I had to sprint to catch him at the exit gate after a flight.

"Whoa... what's the rush, soldier."

"What do you know about a company whose call sign is High Sky?"

He put his flight bag on the floor and looked at his watch, "Man, I have to go... wife has dinner plans." Then let out a long sigh and continued, "I don't know much about it. It's a secretive company, providing a sort of charter to a tech company. I tell you what, I will consult my sources and Wednesday I will disclose everything I learn."

I was bummed. I thought I was going to get all the information I needed on the spot, "Okay... I am just curious."

"When aren't you curious?" He gave me a half smile, slid his bag back on his shoulder and headed to his car, in the employee lot.

Weeks passed and I didn't hear a word from Kevin. I had my first hunch that he was avoiding me, mainly when he called in sick two weeks after our chat in the parking lot.

I searched the Internet for the call sign but didn't get any hits that helped my quest; airline forums were not a big help either.

A month went by and I got a glimpse of Kevin walking away from his plane twice. He pretended he didn't see me, and I decided not to ask again. Then, out of the blue, during a flight, he called me on the radio and asked for my ETA. I gave it to him and he said he was going to wait for me at the airport.

I saw him approaching the airplane as soon as I opened the door."

"Hey," he said with head gesture, "I finally got the information you asked for.

"Oh really," I said, showing interest.

"Yeah... on that matter, I owe you an apology." He said looking up, his right hand as a visor, blocking the sun from reaching his eyes,

"An apology? Because it took so long?"

"Well, yes and no... the more I investigated, the more I liked the company you mentioned... to a point that I saw they had an opening and I applied for it."

"Oh, you did what?"

"Don't worry. I didn't get the job."

"You already interviewed with them?"

"Yep, and I know all the ins and outs to give to you."

I stayed in the cockpit, looking down at him, not sure what to say.

"I must tell you, though, that the opening they had has been filled, and it sounds like those opportunities are very rare. Lots of lifers there."

Should I punch him in the face now or wait a minute?

"I'm so bummed I didn't get the job." He continued, "It is a cool company to work for."

Nerves controlled, I looked at him with the same enthusiasm that someone at looks a plain rock, "Tell me about it."

And so, he did. And yes, the job was the description of my dream job, almost to the tee. The more he talked, the more I understood that his "betrayal" had not been in vain. It became quite clear that it would take a good amount of preparation to apply for such a rare position.

Following the principles that state 'what is good doesn't come easily,' and 'the satisfaction of conquering or getting something is directly proportional to how much work you have to do in order to get it,' it took another 6 years for a job position to open in the local base; but when it did, I jumped on it: scheduled an interview date, rehearsed my answers to all parts of it (personal, professional and technical), got a new suit and a haircut.

Finally, the day came and the interview was a... disaster, to say the least. Three people interviewed me on the spot (one from human resources, the chief pilot – Will - and another pilot) plus the Director of Training was following it through a teleconference arrangement. The guy on the phone was merciless. Every time I got a question right, without stammering, he would say, "I have a follow up question for you..." and his follow-ups were as hard as they get. So, there were a lot of "Uh," "Oh," "Ah," "I don't know the answer for this one," "Frankly, I've never heard about that," and other unsatisfying answers from my side.

The only thing I felt I did right was the approach plate briefing, but by then the '*You are such a fool*' conviction made a full stop landing in my mind.

I left the interview room feeling defeated.

You blew it! You blew your chance. You're such a disgrace. The thought in my head was more ruthless than the phone interviewer.

I left the building a bit disoriented, not even sure where I had parked my cruiser motorcycle. I looked both ways and saw a lonesome bench to my left; a little beyond it, my motorcycle. I walked toward the motorcycle but decided to sit on the bench, for no other reason than to lick my wounds.

I don't know how much time had passed when I was brought back to reality, from my stargazing state, by one of my interviewers.

"Joey... you still here?" Asked Will, the chief pilot. He was about to get in his car when he saw me sitting, with my hands cradling my head, staring to emptiness.

"Uh, uh." *Oh boy, no more that.* "Ah, yes Will. I am collecting my thoughts after my atrocious performance in the interview."

"Yeah, I can't say that it was one of the best I've ever seen," he said while sitting by my side on the bench.

"Is that your polite way of saying it was the worst?"

He laughed, "It wasn't that bad. I had a feeling you knew most of the answers, but had a hard time articulating them."

We started talking and went deeper than any interview could go. He told me about his aviation career, and we exchanged stories of airplanes and people both knew. Forty-five minutes later, he got up, shook my hand vigorously and with a warming smile said, "Well, I have to do something before lunch. We'll stay in touch."

I got up, got on my bike and rode home feeling a little bit better; after all, the experience had not been in vain, I got to meet an accomplished aviator and made a new friend.

I was expecting to hear from the company in about two weeks, with the infamous justification "Thanks for applying, but…"; instead, a week later I got a call from the HR director saying that I had passed the interview process and would be put in a 'pool of pilots,' for when employee attrition happened.

A tangled "okay," was all I managed to get out of my mouth.

Since I didn't know what else to say and the HR person didn't have anything else to say, we hung up. The question marks in my head were so real that I could have used them as ice axes.

Was that a nice way of dismissing me, after the dreadful interview performance?

Life went back to normal and I went back to my cargo flight routine, deciding to forget the whole interview fiasco and hoping that someday they would give me another chance.

Four months later, I had just arrived at my hotel, after my morning cargo flight, and was about to sit down for breakfast when my phone rang. I looked at it and saw that it was the company's HR director.

She didn't waste time with pleasantries and got directly to the point.

"Hey Joey… we have an opening. Would you be able to start a.s.a.p.?"

"What?"

"Someone suddenly quit and we need to send somebody for initial training as soon as we can."

A million thoughts crossed my mind. That's not how I planned to leave the job I had been at for seventeen years.

"Yes… I mean, I need to give my two-week notice."

"We are aware of that. So, could you go for training in two weeks."

No time to ponder.

"Yes?"

"Good… I'm sending your directions by email… there are drug tests and security checks to be accomplished, we have to move fast. Welcome to the company."

BE AMONG THE BEST

When she hung up, my first thought was, *I miss the click made by landlines. Cell phones don't have that kind of closure.*

A moment of exhilaration was mixed with some kind of valediction blues. How was I going to tell my present company that I was going to suddenly leave them, after 17 years of dedication?

The friendliness of my dispatcher didn't make things any easier, "Hi Joey?! How's it going? Everything's good? You never call at this time, any problems with the airplane?"

"Everything's fine, Tim. May I talk with Thomas?"

"Thomas? Ah... sure. Are you alright?"

That single 'yes' felt like a tight knot in my throat. If talking to dispatch was hard, telling the director of operations that these were my last two weeks, felt like betraying a friend.

"I can't ever tell when you are serious." Thomas said, giving me a chance to withdraw the two-week 'joke' notice.

"I am serious now, Thomas."

Long unnerving pause.

"I knew this day would come, someday... but I thought you would give us more time... to find another pilot."

The betrayal felt deeper.

"I thought I would too... but, when an opportunity like this knocks, you don't ask 'who, what or when,' you answer the door by reflex."

"I understand... we will sure miss you."

Ugh! I have never been good at farewells.

Those two weeks flew by, with folks showing (in many ways) that they enjoyed working with me and I should 'come back to visit every now and then.'

The demonstrations of appreciation were so poignant that I was fighting the tears during the last flights, but then, the one that came in the final minutes of my last flight, was the straw that broke the camel's back.

"Capital Tower, Pac 9655, inbound 16 right." The call I had

made thousands of time had reached its end.

It was a cool, idle evening, not many aircraft in the pattern or approach, and the tower controller carried a happy tone and tune, "Welcome home, Pac 9655. You're cleared to land 16 right."

Concentrating on my final checklist, his relaxed clearance made the corners of my mouth go slightly up.

I touched down in the usual spot and let the plane roll to the high-speed taxiway, A9. But when I was about to slightly turn to exit the runway, I saw two fire trucks, one on each side of the intersection of taxiway A and A9. I hadn't noticed them before landing; and now, they were turning their lights on.

That caught me so much by surprise that, in a millisecond, a couple of unpolished thoughts zoomed through my head, *'Am I on fire?'*, *'Is there an aircraft behind me that has declared an emergency,'* *'Is this a drill?'*, and I applied the brakes right away to bring the aircraft to a complete stop, in the middle of the high-speed taxiway.

Before I could formulate what to say to the tower, the words came through my headset, "Go ahead, buddy. This is for you. Thanks for all the years of service for your company."

Those words echoed in my ears, while still trying to make sense of it all, I saw the truck on the right shoot a rainbow of water, the truck on the left followed suit. Then, it dawned on me. It was something I had always wanted... never expecting it to happen so soon.

The water salute is an extraordinary airport tradition to honor military veterans, foreign dignitaries and retiring pilots. Salutes typically involve two firefighting rigs spraying arcs of water over an arriving aircraft. It is a sign of respect, honor and gratitude. It lasts for a couple of minutes and involves a good coordination between ground control and the airport fire department.

Even though it was not my retirement, they knew I wouldn't be flying that operation anymore, at the airport I called home for such a long time. The water salute was a way for the people who worked with me (closely or not) to demonstrate their appreciation.

I taxied under the rainbow of water, my vision blurred, more by the tears than the water on the windshield: one of the happiest moments of my life. I love flying and strive to do my best; and to have my passion recognized by those who surround me, was a grandiose honor.

I pressed the mic, "Thanks guys, it's been a pleasure working with you."

"The pleasure has been ours," ATC's voice sounded emotional too.

A marshaller led me to my parking spot. I went through the shutdown checklist for the last time and noticed a bunch of people coming from the left side. Joe Martinez, my loyal mechanic and dear friend, a tall guy that always seemed to me like a jovial cartoon in real life, was the first one to greet me when the door opened. I was still crying like a child who had just learned he was going to Disneyland.

Joe offered spontaneous consolation, "It's alright, bud. It's alright. We love you." He reinforced his words with a fatherly hug.

"Did you arrange this?"

"'Tweety' did," he said. Greg "Tweety" Thweatt was one of those amazing pilot-friends one finds in the aviation world.

A meteor-question invaded the atmosphere of my mind at once.

Am I doing myself a disfavor by leaving a job where I feel comfortable and appreciated?

I left it in the core of my mind and decided to explore its crater later. Now, it was time for high fives and a farewell party with the group of pilots I had shared life with for so many years.

Two days later, I started a monumental fight against the new beast (a.k.a. simulator) which lasted for twenty days. Twenty days of constant learning how to not only survive, but also tame the beast.

The day I passed my check ride, I met two other pilots with my company that held high positions: the director of operations (Murdock) and one of the company's training captains (Stu). Little did I know, at the time; that these two people would have deep effects in my life. One as an aviation hero; the other, the worst of villains.

The three of us had dinner together. Murdock was chatty while Stu was as quiet as a closed door. I knew Stu was going to be the training captain for my IOE (Initial Operation Experience), and the dinner was an opportunity for me to get introduced to the character I was going to share the cockpit with for the following three weeks.

If the word "introvert" had a face in the dictionary, that would be Stu's. He didn't exchange a single word during the entire dinner. The only eye contact he made was with his fish tacos.

I wonder if this guy is really reserved or truly supercilious?

A week later, I stood in front of a heavy side entrance door to the biggest metal hangar I had ever seen in my life. The company was based in a former Air Force base and the airplanes were kept in a hangar that had been built to accommodate all kinds of airplanes, from Curtiss JN-4 Jennys to B-25 Mitchells, and more recently, K-135s.

KNOCK HARD, VERY HARD. The sign on the door said.

I did and it felt like knocking on a tank. Nobody came. I knocked again, this time, my hand complained.

Normally, you can hear footsteps of someone coming to answer the door. Not with this one, that's why I was stunned by someone suddenly opening it. I was greeted by Stu's smile and firm handshake. For a second, I thought that maybe he had a twin brother or that it was a prank. It turned out that Stu was not only a remarkable guy, but he became the best flight instructor I ever had. And that perception, I soon learned, was a consensus throughout the company.

On the other hand, I noticed that every employee in the company was unquestionably afraid of Murdock, and it took just a few days to understand why.

My positive perceptions went head-to-head against his overbearing personality on the very first trip. During one of the layovers, he started talking trash on the phone about three pilots that everyone else regarded highly, making sure that I could hear him.

When he hung up, he stared at me for a moment, and then said, "Some of these pilots are a royal pain. I have to get rid of them."

In my game, that was strike number one. A legit leader doesn't slam his/her subordinates behind their backs. Later, though, I learned that was the tactic he used to acquire new followers. He was seeking my approval and confidence in order to oust those who didn't agree with him.

The man used dictatorial methods to make the company run smoothly. It was scary to see how a single person was able to exert his power to keep his subordinates swimming straight in a river of fear. It felt like if we stopped paddling or tried to reach the shore, we would all drown.

Strike two happened when I found out that Will, the Chief Pilot who had interviewed me, had left the company because of Murdock. I could clearly imagine the clash of personalities. Will, the level-headed, serene and constructive leader. Murdock, the instigator, the bustling and vengeful ruler. The stress caused by trying to balance the evil, took a toll on Will, and he had to step down to keep his sanity. 'Everyone loves Will' was a pill that Murdock could not swallow.

Then came strike three, and that was a major one because it concerned the area of aviation I treasured the most: Safety.

I could even borrow Dickens' opening to describe it: 'It was

197

the best of times, it was the worst of times.' The best: It was a beautiful clear day, I was healthy and flying for the company I had dreamed of, with pilots that enjoyed being there as much as I did. The worst: I was flying with Murdock.

Our destination airport was famous for being populated by student pilots from other countries, who invariably would confuse ATC instructions. On this occasion, he was the pilot flying and I was the pilot monitoring. We were on a 4-mile final, fully configured and cleared to land, when a trainee aircraft cut us off by turning two miles in front of us, to land.

I saw it right away.

The tower called the trainee aircraft several times, with no response.

"Man, those guys are terrible. Go around." I said as I put one hand on the flaps lever, anticipating his command, and the other hand on the push-to-talk button, ready to let the tower know.

"Nah... no need to go around. If I slow (it) a little bit, we'll be fine."

I thought he was kidding, but there was no kidding with him.

"We are on top of them. Go around." I repeated.

"High Sky, we have an aircraft that is not responding to us and they are just in front of you, on final. I think it is going to be too tight. You guys going around?" The voice of the tower controller came to certify that we had the obvious traffic in sight and were starting our go around.

"Tell him that we are slowing down and will see if the trainee aircraft clears at the first taxiway."

"We're already at Vref (when we should have been Vref+5 knots), this is way too tight." I pleaded.

"You're too new here to judge. We will make it."

I keyed the mike, "Tower, this is Sky High, the captain thinks we have enough trailing space and would like to continue."

"Okay... if you guys are comfortable with it, you may continue.

Cleared to land. Just let me know if you are starting a Go Around."

Oh, I was hoping tower would not accept this option and request us to go around right away.

Our wheels touched down as the trainee aircraft's tail was clearing the first intersection. I bet the tower guy was cringing.

This is it. If I keep flying with this guy, one day we will have a real emergency and he will completely take over, shut me down and try to be a hero. The outcome will not be favorable and I shall regret not being strong enough to voice my concerns earlier.

I vowed to myself to be strong, even if it involved losing the job I enjoyed so much. That was my last flight with Murdock. He probably never figured it out, but my actions and reactions to that episode gave voice to other pilots' concerns.

Less than six months later, 'another job opportunity' was presented to him, and he left. I remember people in the company playing the Wizard of Oz song, 'Ding-dong! The Witch is Dead,' as soon as he walked out of the door.

His departure became the opportunity to make a good company even better. A couple of new positions were created and a new management team took over.

I always thought about countries' governments and the sometimes 'total-lack-of sense' in appointed cabinets. Shouldn't the Secretary of Agriculture have a farming background? Or the Secretary of Education be a professor? Shouldn't the secretary of health be a physician with years of experience?

Our company started operating like an efficient country, with specialized professionals filling the hidden gaps left by Murdock. A lot of dirt and skeletons were found in the closets that he had left behind. It took years for the new team to make them clean and usable again.

The new General Manager was not only an aircraft engineer, who knew our aircraft inside and out, but also a safety (human factors) expert. The new Director of Operations was not only an experienced pilot, but also an aviation lawyer.

And, out of the blue, I was invited to become the new Assistant Chief Pilot. I accepted the position and knew exactly what the first order of business would be. With the help of a couple coworkers, we started a campaign to bring Will back to the company. I had seen him volunteering in an airshow a month prior, and had poked him. He said he would consider it. Then, one month later, and two and a half years after our conversation on the bench, I was 'interviewing' him to come back as our company's Director of Training.

No matter what, good or bad, what goes around really comes around. And in an airplane, it goes and comes even faster.

There's not a single pilot in the entire company that is not better qualified than me, by far. We have top dog pilots that have flown the biggest, fastest and best airplanes in the world. And for the longest time, I questioned the reason why I had been chosen for the position I came to occupy.

The most plausible explanation is simply a joke. If darkness is nothing but the absence of light, would solemnity be the absence of humor? And I can't live without either. That doesn't mean that I don't surely take my job seriously, but what would the world be without "Don't call me, Shirley."

We used to have a layover, for nine crewmembers, at the same time in one of the Bay Area airports, on Tuesdays and Thursdays. We all would "sit" for three hours at the same terminal. Some would go for lunch together, some would exercise and some would take a nap. In any case, we all would change from our uniforms and leave them on hooks attached to the wall, in the storage area that was reserved for us.

During one of these occasions, due to a meeting after my flight, I was the last one to the storage area and noticed that there were seven uniform pants already on the hooks. The seven look alike pants were hanging there so neatly that the light bulb went off right away.

All the crew had gone to lunch, and I was going to meet them at the restaurant after my meeting was over. But before heading their way, I thought it would be funny to switch the order of the pants on the hooks.

After the sit, Jerry, the guy that was flying with me, was the first one to go to change his uniform. I had switched his pants position with the male flight attendant's pants, which were at least two sizes smaller than his. He went in, came out and wait for me to get ready.

On our way to the airplane, he remarked, "I knew I should not have eaten all those chips and that monster burrito. I feel like I am about to explode."

I almost burst out in laughter, but managed to contain myself.

"Yeah... it was a good meal. I feel full too."

We sat in the cockpit and started our pre-flights duties when I spotted the male flight attendant, Benjamin, coming toward the airplane, holding his pants with both hands, like a bride wearing a puffy dress.

He entered the cockpit and said, "One of you guys must be wearing my pants."

"What?" said Jerry.

Benjamin pointed to Jerry's pants and said, "Those are mine."

"How do you know?" I ask.

"The belt... that's my buckle! Jerry, did you switch our pants on the hooks."

"I am wearing someone else's pants too." I said, but I really wasn't.

"What the heck is happening here?" Jerry said, "That's why I am bursting out of these. Let's go to the back of the airplane and switch back."

201

"There's one problem." Benjamin said in a lower voice.

"What?"

"I went running…"

"You went running wearing my pants?"

"No, silly. I went running, and took a shower."

"And…"

"I forgot to pack a clean pair of underwear." Benjamin confessed.

"What? Are you telling me that you are wearing your sweaty underwear under MY pants?" Jerry was getting exasperated.

"Worse than that." Benjamin was flushing.

"Uh?"

"I'm commando!"

"Gross." I said, while Jerry buried his face in his crossed arms and yelled, "Noooo!!"

They went to the restroom and exchanged pants. The other pilots were able to figure out the switch before things got out of hand.

The word spread around about Jerry and Benjamin's pants exchange and the other crew members still give them a hard time. I blamed the prank on a female flight attendant that likes to joke too. No one was ever able to confirm the mastermind… until now.

Life is too short not to have a good laugh, but can also become short if we don't take our job seriously.

Every day, we strive to be better, to work quietly not to make the 8 o'clock headline, in a world where only negative outcomes make news, to improve the lives of the people we touch and to put a smile on the face of the people that may not even know about us. Our excellence is found in the constant pursuit of perfection, but it doesn't dwell in its achievement. If you want to be great, you ought to infiltrate the world of the best.

CHAPTER TWENTY-FOUR

Epilogue

I once read a message written by a sage old man, on his deathbed, titled, "If I had to live my life all over again," where he described everything he regretted doing or not doing and how he would live his life if he had a chance to redo it.

After I finished reading it, I couldn't help but thinking about my own life.

Ah… what would I change in my passage on Earth?

I considered a couple of episodes that I wish I hadn't gone through, but then, I reconsidered the thought. I wouldn't change anything, even the most painful moments. Why? Because it wouldn't be me writing these words anymore. A small change then, would mean a big change now; that's what some people call "the Butterfly effect." Forget the possibilities lost; they only lead to conclusions of a perfectly unfounded present.

If you are a professional pilot who travels to/from your base, I bet you have gone through this scenario. You are commuting/deadheading in your uniform, sitting among regular passengers, and the person next to you asks, "Shouldn't you be in the cockpit, flying the airplane?" When you finish explaining the situation, as you've done hundreds of times, the person says, "I wish I were a pilot. As a matter of fact, I did have a chance to do it, but it was too hard."

My reply to this wishful thinking is always the same, "You're never too old, to do anything you want to do."

The person normally shakes his head and whispers to himself or herself, "It's too late for me."

I conclude our short exchange by saying, "An unhappy life is not only harder, but also bitter."

People make excuses not-to-be-happy, as if happiness were to be feared.

You will make mistakes, like flying to Carlson City, Chino and Yreka, when you should have landed in Crescent City, Chico and Eureka. By the way, it wasn't me; I only witnessed those blunders happening, more than once. Fool me once, shame on you; fool me twice, Shane (the dispatcher) gets you fired.

Just be smart in picking your risks, avoid the stupid ones. I picked a lot of stupid ones, thanks to my inability to refuse a dare. Some of the stupid risks were kind of innocent:

I had just got to the Eureka airport, and a bunch of pilots were gathered at the counter, giggling. One of the guys looked toward me and I heard him saying, "I bet Joey would do it."

"Do what?"

"Keep a seed from this Ghost Pepper in your mouth for one minute."

Needless to say, I ended up with blisters inside my lower lips, and it even hurt to speak on the radio.

Other ventures were not so innocent:

"We need to get these passengers to Neverland. The other pilots are refusing to go because there is a small Squall Line approaching the destination. We need a real pilot."

"I will take it." Those words could have been my last ones. The idiocy of a pilot is inversely proportional to his flying age. Naivete kills more pilots than engine failures ever will.

Even a life-and-death situation is better than endangering

lives. After so many lessons learned, one evening, during the peak cargo season, I was loaded and ready to go, and said the words that no operator ever wants to hear from its pilots.

"I am not going!"

"Say what?" the loaders were shocked. One of them went to the manager's office to break the news. The manager came running to me.

"Joey... I heard you don't want to go HOME?" He strategically put that word at the end, and continued, "It's not THAT bad. I have seen you flying in worse weather than this."

It started raining even harder, and I pulled the chair I was perched on and moved it to the shelter created by the hangar door.

"It's getting worse by the second. The winds are not bad here... but as soon as I leave the ground, they will throw me against the mountains."

"C'mon, Joey. That's nonsense."

As he finished saying that, we heard the noise of a helicopter engine. A rescue helicopter came and touched down on the main ramp, not far from us. The pilot did not shut down his engine; we all saw one person running to the terminal, and seconds later, three people running toward the helicopter. They got in and the helicopter took off.

The manager and the ramp workers looked at me with exclamation points on their faces, like, "Even a helicopter is taking off!"

They got even more upset when I didn't make any effort to move or say anything. I stood my ground.

Ten minutes later, a witness, on the ground, reported hearing a helicopter flying very low over her house, just above the 100-foot-tall treetops. She said there were strong gusts and heavy rain. Two miles later, the helicopter was slammed against the mountain wall while trying to get back to the airport. No one survived.

Contrary to the popular saying, I believe that there are old, bold pilots; but their boldness is inversely proportional to their experience.

Aviation is an art that demands a level of constant precision, associated with correct decisions. It allows you to learn with your own small mistakes, and with other aviators' big errors. And as long as you can get back home with an old tail and a new tale, you will be rewarded with the gift of being able to reach the skies another day.

We are all living with some form of present we would like to give - some special expression of thrill, creativity or spirit of live that we are hiding under our coat. I hope this book inspires you to tell your own stories to the world. You may not know it, but they are ready to be told. The act of sharing makes us more. Relive them by revealing them.

Happy tales.

CPSIA information can be obtained
at www.ICGtesting.com
Printed in the USA
LVHW020012080222
710483LV00014B/622